Just the Facts!
Winning Endgame Knowledge In One Volume

by
GM Lev Alburt
and GM Nikolay Krogius

Published by:
Chess Information and Research Center

For ordering information, please see page 412.

Distribution to the book trade by:
W.W. Norton, 500 Fifth Avenue, New York, NY

Staff:

Editing & Design	OutExcel! Corporation Al Lawrence, President
Art Director	Jami L. Anson
Art Consultant	Lev Maximov
Editorial Consultants	Peter Kurzdorfer Jonathan Crumiller
Cover	Mark Kostabi's painting "Red Handed"
Drawings	Jami L. Anson
Photos courtesy	The Chess Cafe www.chesscafe.com U.S. Chess Federation www.uschess.com Bill Hook
Computer Analysis	ChessBase USA www.chessbaseusa

ISBN: 1-889323-06-3
Library of Congress Catalog Card Number: 99-066852

10 9 8 7 6 5 4 3 2 1

Printed in the United States of America.

Note to Reader

You should be able to read a chess book without squinting, without forever flipping pages back and forth to find the relevant diagram, and without trying to keep a 12-move variation in your head. We've tried to produce *Just the Facts! Winning Endgame Knowledge in One Volume* in a way that makes it enjoyable for you to get the most out of the unique instruction it contains. Lots of diagrams make it easier. And look for color-coded diagrams and "break-outs" that call your attention to the most important positions and ideas. These will be especially worth revisiting and even committing to memory.

A special note on notation and ranks

Just the Facts! uses the now universal algebraic notation. In the text, however, when we discuss general rules—such as rooks belonging on their seventh rank or the king being cut off on its fourth rank—we fall back on the English descriptive tradition of relative perspective. This technique is so widely used in both conversation and writing that it will come naturally to readers, and it obviates the use of tedious and confusing repetition ("The second rank for White, or the seventh for Black," etc.).

For more on notation, see volume 1 of the *Comprehensive Chess Course*.

Introduction

"Just the facts, ma'am."

—*Detective Joe Friday of the popular 1950s* Dragnet
*television series, to countless crime witnesses
tempted to stray from the essential points of the case.*

We've taken our cue from Jack Webb's famous *Dragnet* detective. In a hurry to solve a case, he wanted witnesses to give him quickly "Just the facts." We know that's what you want when you sit down to spend your precious free time to improve your chess.

Providing "just the facts" of all the endings you're likely to encounter in a lifetime of chess was a considerable challenge. It required the team of famous player, writer, and teacher GM Lev Alburt and renowned endgame expert and trainer GM Nikolay Krogius. Their decades of both championship-level play and teaching on all levels, and their keen interest in producing the most helpful material possible, led to a uniquely effective approach.

The endgame is the last lap in the race for chess victory. In another sports analogy, C.J.S Purdy called the ending the "putting" of chess. Joe Friday might have said it was the perpetrator's court conviction that served as the epilogue of every episode of *Dragnet*. Whatever the metaphor, it's clear that, depending on your endgame knowledge, you can either enjoy the victory your hours of concentration in the opening and middlegame have earned you, or you can spoil it all. If you know some basic ideas and techniques, you can even save some "lost" games. Such climaxes and anti-climaxes happen over and over in every chess tournament.

The best news is that your endgame play can improve dramatically in a very short time—with the proper help. And a real knowledge of endgame play will never go out of fashion. Here you have the essential ideas, principles and positions. *Just the Facts!* will serve you well through many, many years of chessboard battles.

Just the Facts! Winning Endgame Knowledge in One Volume is the final volume of the *Comprehensive Chess Course,* a series that has earned a special status with chess players. Each of its books has been a widely praised best seller since first publication. That's because each book is a careful distillation and *explanation* of hundreds of years of master practice and teaching.

The entire series focuses on making the most effective use of your time. Only the important ideas are included. No sidetracks down theoretical curiosities. No long, unexplained lines that leave you scratching your head and looking at your watch. No asides that will lead you to a Jack Webb staccato-like "Just the facts!" See page 412 of this book to order volumes of the course.

After the hard work and high expectations, we're very proud that the seventh World Chess Champion, Vassily Smyslov, could write: "The right endgame knowledge is the magic key to chess mastery. *Just the Facts!* gives you that key!"

Al Lawrence, Executive Editor
Former Executive Director of the U.S. Chess Federation

Table of Contents

Just the Facts!

Winning Endgame Knowledge in One Volume

Chapter 1: What *Is* an Endgame?   **10**
◆Endgame knowledge—the key to chess mastery   12
◆The active king   13
◆Passed pawns   19
◆Zugzwang   25
◆Summary   28

Chapter 2: Pawn Endings   **30**
Part 1: King Position   32
◆King and one pawn versus king—the fundamentals   32
◆Chess is a game for squares   34
◆How to win a pawn up: Three rules for   37
    battling a blocking king
◆Most Winnable Endgames—   41
    the more pawns, the more winnable!
◆Rook pawns—when living on the edge can be safe   46
◆Defending by jailing the opposing   46
    king on the rook's file
◆Safe squares   51
◆Passing the move (triangulation)   52
◆Calling in the reserves (reserve pawn moves)   53
◆The moving screen   56
◆The distant opposition   58
◆A classic triangulation   62
Part II: Passed Pawns   64
◆The advantage of the outside passed pawns   64
◆Mutual defense treaties between pawns   69
◆Creating passed pawns—radical breakthroughs   74
◆Summary   79
◆Learning Exercises   80

Chapter 3: Pawns against Pieces   **82**
◆Pawn versus knight   83
◆When the lone horseman holds off   86
   both king and rook pawn
◆You can't *always* win   88
◆Bishop versus pawns   105
◆Rook against pawn   114
◆Cutting off the king on his third rank   115
◆The running screen in rook-versus-pawn endings   118
◆Two connected pawns versus the rook   120
◆Queen versus pawns   126
◆Summary   133
◆Learning Exercises   134

Chapter 4: Rook Endings   **136**
◆Rook and pawn versus rook, with the defending   138
   king blocking the pawn
   Pawn is on the sixth rank   138
   Pawn is not yet on the sixth rank—Philidor's position   140
◆Lucena's position   143
◆Counterattacking from the side—   146
   the long-side defense
◆When the long side is too short   151
◆The defending king is cut off from the pawn   152
◆When the extra pawn is a rook-pawn   155
◆Rook versus rook and two pawns   161
◆Special case of the rook- and bishop-pawns   162
◆Rook and pawns versus rook and pawns   163
◆Beware of passive defense   173
◆Summary   181
◆Learning Exercises   182

Chapter 5: Knight Endings   **184**
◆Knight and pawn against knight   188
◆The king takes part in the defense   193
◆Both sides have pawns, and one is passed   197
◆Wing majorities   200
◆Importance of the active king   202
◆Summary   205
◆Learning Exercises   206

Chapter 6: Bishop Endings **208**
Part 1: Bishops of the Same Color 210
◆Pawn on the sixth or seventh rank 210
◆Pawn not yet on the sixth or seventh rank 212
◆Bishop and two pawns against bishop 217
◆Both sides have pawns—the "bad" bishop 220
◆Both sides have pawns—the "good" bishop 224
◆Same-Color Bishops: Drawing and Winning Methods 225
◆Other strategies 226
Part 2: Bishops of Opposite Color 228
◆Good fortresses require bad bishops! 229
◆Passed pawns 229
◆Don't overburden your bishop 233
◆It's not *always* a draw! 234
◆Fortress Building and Maintenance 101 235
◆Connected passed pawns—the three rules of defense 240
◆Targeting 244
◆Summary 246
◆Learning Exercises 248

Chapter 7: Knight against Bishop **250**
◆Play with one pawn on the board 251
◆Play with multiple pawns 262
◆The knight can be the "Springer of surprises"! 270
◆The knight can be stronger in close quarters 271
and closed positions
◆The knight against the bad bishop 275
◆Summary 281
◆Learning Exercises 282

Chapter 8: Queen Endings **284**
◆ Queen and pawn against queen 287
◆ Queens and multiple pawns 294
◆ Summary 307
◆ Learning Exercises 308

Chapter 9: Mixed Bags **310**
◆Basic checkmates 311
◆Bishop and knight 312
◆Two knights against a pawn 312
◆Focus on practicality 313
◆Rook versus knight with no pawns on the board 313

◆Don't stand in the corner!   315
◆Rook versus knight with pawns on the board   317
◆Rook versus bishop   319
◆Rook and pawn versus bishop   321
◆Rook and pawns versus bishop and pawns   324
◆Rook and bishop versus rook   329
◆Queen versus rook   334
◆Queen versus rook and non-rook pawn   337
◆Queen versus rook and rook pawn   337
◆Queen versus rook and minor piece   343
◆Summary   349
◆Learning Exercises   350

Chapter 10: Multi-Piece Endings   **352**
◆Advantage of the bishop pair   353
◆Two rooks versus two rooks   360
◆The importance of a spatial advantage   364
◆Creating additional weaknesses   369
◆Summary   373
◆Learning Exercises   375

Chapter 11: Transitions   **376**
◆Playing for a favorable ending from move four   378
◆Heading for the endgame as a defensive measure   395
◆Summary   402
◆The Relative Value of the Pieces Change   403
   in the Endgame!
◆Learning Exercises   404

Conclusion   **406**
A Brief Endgame Glossary   **408**

Key to Commonly Used Chess Symbols

#	checkmate	!?	interesting move
+	check	?!	dubious move
++	double check	=	an equal position
!	excellent move	±	White is better
!!	outstanding move	∓	Black is better
?	weak move	+-	White is winning
??	blunder	-+	Black is winning

Chapter 1: What *Is* an Endgame?
Some Important Ideas to Look For

◆ Triumphant penetration of the king
White plays 6. Ka7.
See Diagram 2.

◆ Power of the passed pawn
Black plays 1. ... Rxb2!.
See Diagram 12.

◆ The winning power of zugzwang
White plays 1. Ke4!.
See Diagram 19.

◆ The drawing power of zugzwang
White plays Ke6!.
See Diagram 21.

Chapter 1
What Is an Endgame?

Three Distinguishing Characteristics

You'd think that something so widely studied and discussed as the chess endgame would be commonly well defined. Sometimes it's described simply as the final stage of a chess game. This definition isn't accurate. Many games finish before they ever reach an endgame—for example, when a player resigns or is checkmated in the middlegame, or when he blunders fatally in the opening. The exchange of queens is often heralded as the onset of the endgame. But this is an oversimplification. There are endgames with queens and there are middle games without them.

Perhaps it's better to define the endgame simply as the stage of the game with relatively few pieces on the board. Beyond this generalized definition, there are three distinguishing characteristics that can help us to both recognize the endgame and at the

same time play better when we reach one:
- ♚ Endgames favor an aggressive king;
- ♚ The importance of passed pawns is greatly increased in the endgame;
- ♚ Zugzwang—the "compulsion to move" when doing so forces a player into a worsened or even losing position—is often a factor in the endgame while almost unheard of in the other stages.

In this chapter, we'll take a look at each of these key characteristics in turn.

ENDGAME KNOWLEDGE——THE KEY TO CHESS MASTERY

Former World Champion Vassily Smyslov has called the endgame "the magic key to chess mastery." We hear and read constantly of new subtleties in the opening said to confer an important advantage. The unexpected combinations and sacrificial attacks of the middlegame excite our fighting spirit and imagination. Why not just concentrate on these two phases? Regretably, too many players fall into just that very trap. They shortchange their endgame knowledge by spending all of their time for chess on the first two parts of the game.

> *If you want to win at chess, begin with the ending.*
> —*Irving Chernev*

But any truly good player or coach will tell you that an approach that ignores the endgame is both illogical and impractical. As we'll see throughout this book, many middlegame plans—and, occasionally even opening strategies—have the goal of creating favorable endings. Without practical endgame skill, you won't be able to realize the opening or middlegame advantage you fought so hard to achieve.

With knowledge of the basic endgame techniques, you can enjoy the victory you've spent the whole game earning. At times, you'll even be able to pull yourself free of the steely jaws

OF THE THREE PHASES OF THE GAME— OPENING, MIDDLEGAME AND END- GAME, THE ENDGAME HAS THE LEAST IN COMMON WITH ITS FELLOW STAGES IN TERMS OF PRINCIPLES GUIDING CORRECT PLAY. IN FACT, SOME RULES GOOD IN THE OPENING AND MIDDLEGAME REVERSE THEMSELVES IN THE ENDGAME!

of "certain" defeat. And, as the great world champion Jose Capablanca was fond of pointing out, no stage of the game reveals the true powers of the pieces as does the endgame. Those who study the endgame know the essence of chess.

THE ACTIVE KING

To be a winning endgame general, you must know the key differences between the ending and the other phases of the game, the opening and middlegame. The critical distinction is that, in the endgame, the king often becomes an active, even an aggressive piece. The sacred middlegame commandment enjoining you to protect your king at all costs loses its sanctity in the endgame, where the king attacks pawns and pieces and is often first to penetrate the opponent's position.

Let's look at two examples that illustrate the active role of a king in endings.

In Diagram 1, White's chances are better because he has the two bishops and an extra pawn on the queenside. Despite these advantages, after 1. ... Nc4 2. Bc1 Rc7, Black could reasonably hope for a successful defense. But the line Black chose in the game allowed the White king to penetrate the queenside.

The king is a strong piece—use it!
—Reuben Fine

SVESHNIKOV—BROWNE
WIJK AN ZEE, 1981

Black should play 1. ... Nc4 2. Bc1 Rc7. You can learn from his mistake.

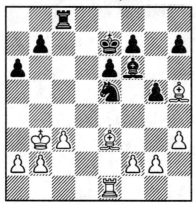

Diagram 1
Black to move

1. ... Nd3? 2. Rd1 Nc5+

Better was 2. ... Ne5. As often happens, one mistake begets another.

3. Kb4! Ne4

If 3. ... b6, then White plays 4. a4, with the threat of 5. a5.

4. Ka5 Nd6 5. Kb6 Rc6+ 6. Ka7

Diagram 2

A triumphal march of the king! Now Black can't protect his pawns.

6. ... Rc7 7. Bb6 Rc6 8. Ba5 Be5 9. Bf3 Rc5 10. Bb4 Rc7

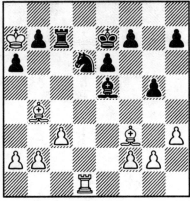

Diagram 3

11. Kb6!

White correctly delays capturing the pawn on b7.

11. ... Rd7 12. Re1 f6 13. a4 Kd8 14. Bxd6 Rxd6+ 15. Kxb7

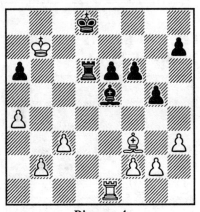

Diagram 4

White has a passed c-pawn, and a potential passed pawn as its neighbor. These guarantee White an easy win.

15. ... Rd2 16. Rd1 Rxd1 17. Bxd1 a5 18. Kb6 Bc7+ 19. Kc6

**THE FIRST CRUCIAL DIFFERENCE
BETWEEN THE ENDGAME
AND OTHER STAGES:
ENDGAMES FAVOR
AN AGGRESSIVE KING!**

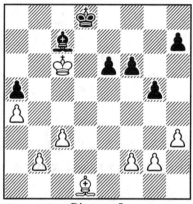

Diagram 5

**19. ... Bf4 20. Kb7 Be5 21. Be2 Bd6 22. g3 f5 23.
Kc6 Bb8 24. Bc4 e5 25. b4**

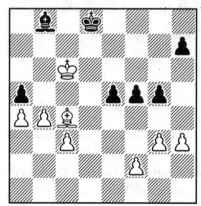

Diagram 6

**25. ... Ba7 26. Kb7 Bxf2 27. bxa5 Bxg3 28. a6 Bf2
29. Be6**

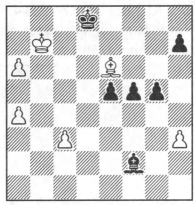

Diagram 7

Neutralizing Black's passers.

29. ... f4 30. Bd5 h5 31. Bf3, Black resigns.

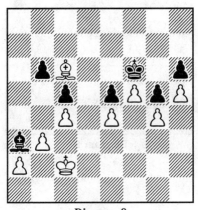

Diagram 8
White to move

White's king must penetrate Black's position to attack the pawns at b6 and h6. Black's pawns and bishop block his way. But White can sacrifice to create a path for his king.

1. b4! Bxb4

If 1. ... cxb4, then 2. Kb3 Bc1 3. Kxb4 Be3 4. Kb5 Ke7 5. Bd5 Bg1 6. a4 Bd4 7. c5! bxc5 (or 7. ... Bxc5 8. a5) 8. Bc4 and White will queen one of his pawns.

Diagram 9
After 8. Bc4

2. Kb3 Ba5 3. Ka4 Ke7 4. Kb5 Kf6 5. Bd5 Ke7

Diagram 10

6. Kc6

Zugzwang.

6. ... Kf6 7. Kd7 Bc3 8. a4 Ba5 9. Ke8

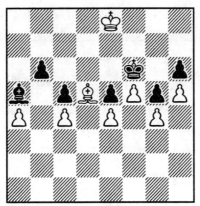

Diagram 11

9. ... b5

Or else White plays 10. Kf8-g8-h7xh6. If 9. ... Kg7
then 10. Ke7.

10. axb5 Bc7 11. Kd7, Black resigns.

PASSED PAWNS

Passed pawns play an increasingly important role in the
endgame, often determining victory or defeat. In the middlegame, only a piece or two of the
many on the board may
decide the outcome. But in
the endgame, all the pieces
are likely to be engaged.
and their activity
sometimes cen-
ters on for-
warding
or stopping a
passed pawn.

ORTUETA—SANZ
MADRID, 1934

Diagram 12
Black to move

At first glance there is no serious threat to White's position and the outcome should most likely be a draw. But …

1. ... Rxb2! 2. Nxb2 c3 3. Rxb6

Or 3. Nd3 c4 + 4. Rxb6 cxd3, and the Black pawns are unstoppable.

Diagram 13

3. ... c4!

Co-Author: International Grandmaster
Lev Alburt

Place of Birth: Orenburg, Russia
Date of Birth: August 21, 1945

GM Alburt lived for many years in Odessa, a Ukrainian city located on the Black Sea. He won the highly competitive Ukraine championship three times, in 1972-1974. He won the European Cup Championship twice, in 1976 and 1979.

Renowned player, teacher and writer

Mentored by world champion & pre-eminent teacher Mikhail Botvinnik

◆ Three-time US Champion: 1984,1985, 1990

◆ Twice US Open Champion: 1987, 1989

◆ Three-time Ukraine Champion: 1972-74

◆ Popular *Chess Life* Columnist

◆ Sought after teacher

◆ Architect of best selling *Comprehensive Chess Course*

In the days when there were still a Berlin wall and a tight KGB-guard on "Soviet" GMs, Alburt defected while at a tournament in then West Germany.

In 1979, he came to the U.S., making his home in New York City. He won the U.S. Championship an impressive three times–in 1984, 1985 and 1990.

Famous for providing aspiring players easy access to master-level ideas, Alburt is the only top-echelon GM to devote his career to teaching non-masters. His *Comprehensive Chess Course*, of which this book is the seventh and final volume, is a long-time best seller.

He provides lessons through-the-mail, over-the-telephone, and face-to-face. Write to GM Lev Alburt at PO Box 534, Gracie Station, New York, NY, 10028, or call him at (212) 794-8706.

This star move takes the d3-square away from White, and threatens 4. ... c2. That's why White responded ...

4. Rb4 a5! 5. Na4

If 5. Rb5, then 5. ... c2. And if 5. Rxc4, then ... cxb2.

5. ... axb4, White resigns.

An effective demonstration of the power of the far-advanced passed pawns!

KROGIUS—DOROSHKEVICH
KAZAN, 1964

Diagram 14
White to move

White's position looks hopeless, but the Exchange sacrifice allows him to create a dangerous passed pawn. The game continued:

1. Rxd4! cxd4 2. c5 Ne4

To stop the pawn: 2. ... Nxb3 leads to a drawish queen and knight versus queen ending.

3. c6 Kg6

Or 3. ... d3 4. c7 d2 5. c8(Q) d1(Q) 6. Qb7+, with a drawish queen ending.

4. c7 Nd6 5. Kf3 Kf5 6. h4 Ke6 7. h5

Now Black has to switch his attention to another passed pawn.

7. ... Kf5

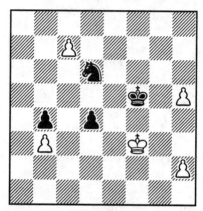

Diagram 15

8. h6 Kg6 9. c8(Q)

The try 9. Kf4 Kxh6 10. Ke5 d3 11. Kxd6 d2 would also lead to a draw.

9. ... Nxc8 10. Ke4 Ne7 11. Kxd4 Nc6+ 12. Kc5 Ne5, draw.

In some cases, a passed pawn can successfully oppose major pieces—a rook or even a queen.

THE SECOND SIGNIFICANT DIFFERENCE BETWEEN THE ENDGAME AND THE OTHER STAGES OF THE CHESS GAME IS THE GREATLY INCREASED IMPORTANCE OF PASSED PAWNS.

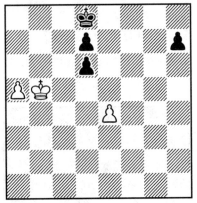

Diagram 16
White to move

In this endgame study by Troitsky, White draws with:

1. Kb6! Kc8

Otherwise, a pawn will queen.

**2. a6 Kb8 3. a7+ Ka8 4. Kc7 h5 5. Kxd6 h4 6. Kxd7 h3
7. e5 h2 8. e6 h1(Q) 9. e7**

Diagram 17

9. ... Qd5+ 10. Kc7 Qe6 11. Kd8 Qd6+ 12. Kc8!

Diagram 18

12. ... Qc6+

On 12. ... Qxe7, it's stalemate.

13. Kd8 Kb7 14. a8(Q)+!

If White plays 14. e8(Q)?, then 14. ... Qc7 checkmate!

14. ... Kxa8 15. e8(Q), draw.

> *A passed pawn increases in strength as the*
> *number of pieces on the board diminishes.*
> *—Jose Capablanca*

ZUGZWANG

Because of the small number of pieces in the endgame, play often takes on a very forceful character, with every move, every tempo increasingly important. On the other hand, the choice of acceptable variations gets narrowed, sometimes leading to a situation in which one of the sides exhausts all useful moves and would like to simply "sit" on the position he's built.

WHEN A PLAYER MUST MOVE, BUT ANY MOVE WORSENS HIS POSITION, HE IS SAID TO BE IN *ZUGZWANG*. AT SUCH A MOMENT THE PLAYER WANTS TO "PASS." BUT, ALAS, PASSING IS NOT PERMITTED IN CHESS. A PLAYER MUST MOVE!

FOLTYS—MAKARCHIK
WARSAW, 1949

Diagram 19
White to move

1. Ke4!

Black is in zugzwang—the compulsion to move. He doesn't have any moves that would prevent the White rook's moving from a8 with check, allowing the promotion of the a7-pawn to a queen.

This is the perfect example of all three themes—zugzwang, the importance of passed pawns, and the active king—all working together.

Diagram 20
White to move

In this study, White is a pawn down and struggling for a draw. He gets his wish by sacrificing his only pawn.

1. Kf5 Kg7 2. e7 Kf7 3. e8(Q)+! Kxe8 4. Ke6!

THE THIRD SIGNIFICANT DIFFERENCE OF AN ENDGAME FROM THE OTHER STAGES OF THE GAME: ZUGZWANG IS A FREQUENT FACTOR IN THE ENDGAME. ZUGZWANG NEVER TAKES PLACE IN THE OPENING AND IS EXTREMELY RARE IN THE MIDDLEGAME.

Diagram 21

Only this move, which forces Black into a zugzwang, leads to a draw. If 4. Kxf6? Kd7 5. Kf5 Kc6 6. Ke4 Kc5 7. Kd3 Kd5, and Black is winning. Now, however, Black cannot make constructive use of his material advantage. For example ...

4. ... Kd8 5. Kxd6 or 4. ... f5 5. Kxf5 Kd7 6. Ke4 Kc6 7. Kd4

We arrive at a well known drawn position.

Summary: Paradoxically, chess games can end without an "endgame." Endgames aren't easy to define—for example they can sometimes involve queens on the board. Still there are three defining characteristics that make them very different from the opening or middlegame: endgames often favor an active king; passed pawns greatly increase in importance, and zugzwang can become a factor. You should make time to learn basic endgame techniques. Seventh World Chess Champion Vassily Smyslov pointed out that "the right endgame knowledge is the magic key to chess mastery."

Krogius the year his team won the World Student Team Championship

Central in training a whole generation of dominant Soviet GMs

◆ Special trainer to World Champion Boris Spassky

◆ Russian Federation Champion

◆ Repeated winner of the prestigious Sochi and Varna International Tournaments

◆ Doctorate in psychology

◆ Renowned endgame expert

Place of Birth: Saratov, Russia
Date of Birth: July 22, 1930

GM Nikolay Krogius is a famed endgame expert, renowned trainer, and pioneering chess psychologist. He is so highly valued that World Champion Boris Spassky, in his 1972 defense against Bobby Fischer, insisted on Krogius as a special coach. Krogius helped train a famous generation of Soviet players who still dominate world chess.

Krogius became a grandmaster in 1964. Among other impressive results as a player, he was co-champion of the Russian Federation in 1952 (along with Aronin) and has placed first in a long list of the prestigious international tournaments—among which are Varna, 1960; Sochi, 1964 (ahead of Spassky); Sochi, 1969 (equal with Spassky and Zaitsev); and Varna, 1969 (ahead of Hort).

For more than 10 years, Krogius was in charge of the entire Soviet chess juggernaut. He is the author of a number of highly praised books on the endgame and chess psychology.

Nikolay Krogius now lives in Brooklyn.

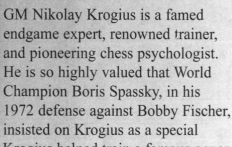

Chapter 2: Pawn Endings
Some Important Ideas to Look For

◆ Barricades & the Rule of the Square

White's on move, but is blocked.
See Diagram 29.

◆ The "moving screen"

White plays 2. Kd5.
See Diagram 60.

◆ Losing a move to win the game

White plays Kd5-Kc4-Kd4-Kd5.
See Diagram 68.

◆ Breakthrough thinking

White plays 2. h4! and queens.
See Diagram 87.

Chapter 2
Pawn Endings:
Atomic Chess

Pawn endings are the irreducible wins, losses, and draws of chess. They are the atoms of chess physics, the foundation of endgame play. Nearly all ending positions can melt down, sometimes quite suddenly, into a pawn endgame. So your endgame play must take into account the possibility of a sudden reduction of forces to one of these fundamental, atomic positions— and what your fate would be if this happened. The good news is that you don't have to be an atomic physicist to play these endings like a master!

There are two principal features that determine play in any pawn ending—the position of the kings and the presence of passed pawns. These two features intertwine in practice. But it will help us to focus on them separately. In Part I, we'll spotlight the king positions. Then in Part II we'll concentrate on the role of passed pawns.

Part I: King Position
King and one pawn vs. king
—— The Fundamentals

Let's start by looking at the basic positions where king and pawn oppose a lone king. Your knowledge of the small diagrams that follow will often determine your game plan with more pawns on the board. These endings are common and the superior side wins only about 50% of the time, so you can save many games by knowing some simple defensive techniques. White wants simply to queen his pawn, when mate would follow easily and quickly. From a defender's point of view, the crucial two fundamentals are a "one or the other approach" that's easy to master and remember.

♟ If the enemy pawn can be attacked and captured before queening and before the opposing king can support it, then that's the obvious choice. Let's take a look at this simple process.

Diagram 22

Here the superior side's king is too far away to support his pawn, and the defending king can get to it before it queens. Black draws easily, no matter who moves first, by moving toward the White pawn and capturing it. If it's Black's move, 1. ... Kf5 does the trick. The only losing idea would be to move the king farther away from and "below" the pawn, allowing the foot soldier to get an uncatchable lead—for example, 1. ... Kf4. If it's White's move, Black still plays 1. ... Kf5, unless White first plays 1. e6, when 1. ... Kf6 guarantees the extermination of the pawn.

♟ If the pawn can be supported in time by its king, so that it can't simply be captured, then the defending king must get in front of the pawn—such blocking is the only hope. But this simple strategy, when correctly followed up, frequently draws.

Here's an example of a basic position illustrating the importance of blocking—a technique that you should internalize as defensive instinct.

Diagram 23

With Black to move, he draws with 1. ... Ke6, getting immediately into the path of the pawn. If, as many beginning players will do, he plays 1. ... Ke4 to "attack" the pawn immediately, he loses! White would play 2. Kc4, eventually queening the pawn. (Volume 2 of the *Comprehensive Chess Course* thoroughly covers such ending fundamentals. See page 412.)

WHEN DEFENDING, MOVE YOUR KING IN FRONT OF THE PAWN—*BLOCKING* IS THE ONLY HOPE. THIS SIMPLE STRATEGY, WHEN CORRECTLY FOLLOWED UP, FREQUENTLY DRAWS.

Diagram 24   **Diagram 25**

You can't stop a pawn from the side. Block it!

You can't stop the pawn from behind. Block it!

CHESS IS A GAME FOR SQUARES

Many times in king-and-pawn endings, it's necessary to know whether a king can catch an unsupported pawn breaking for its eighth rank. Of course, when the king and pawn are close to each other, you can quickly play out each move in your head—the pawn goes here, the king moves there. But when the king and pawn are farther apart, such a method takes time and can lead to errors, so we need a better technique. One method is called "counting." You count the number of moves the pawn needs to reach the queening square and then count how many moves the king requires. If the pawn moves first, the king will arrive in time if it requires an equal number, or fewer, moves.

There's even a simpler method by which, with a little practice, you can tell at a glance who'll win the race. It presumes that the king is unblocked from its shortest path. (If the king faces obstacles, the counting method is best.) It's called the rule of the square. There's probably no single more important calculation tool in the endgame. Although it's taught all over the world, credit is hardly ever given to the 19th-century Austrian player and writer who invented this fundamental tool—Johann Berger. (He's the same fellow who invented a tie-breaking system for chess tournaments. Too bad for Johann that he didn't have a friendly patent office in his native Graz!)

Berger pointed out, and Tarrasch popularized the idea, that you could simply imagine an equal-sided box drawn from the pawn's current square to its promotion square. Draw the square toward the king. If the king is within the square, or on move can get into the square, he can catch the pawn. If he can't, he'll lose the race. No calculating or counting necessary! Just be careful if the pawn is in its original position, and take into account its first-move option of leaping two squares forward.

Diagram 26
Black to move
The king catches the pawn.

Diagram 27
White or Black to move
The pawn will queen.

From Diagram 26, with Black to move, his king enters the square, catches and captures the pawn, drawing: 1. ... Kf4 2. b5 Ke5 3. b6 Kd6 4. b7 Kc7. With White to move, he wins by advancing the pawn out of reach of the defending king.

From Diagram 27, Black is lost, whoever is to move.

IF THE KING, ON MOVE, CAN ENTER THE SQUARE, IT CAN CATCH THE PAWN IN TIME.

But sometimes the presence of other pawns can complicate the issue of whether a king can catch an enemy passed pawn.

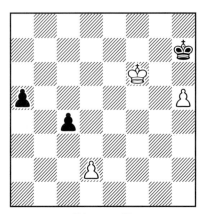

Diagram 28
White to move

1. Ke5

It seems that the passed pawn could be easily stopped—after all, the king is within the square. However, Black has a trick that blocks the White king's path.

1. ... c3! 2. dxc3 a4 3. Kd4 a3

Diagram 29

Black's pawn now queens easily.

Here's an example where the "tricks" help the defender.

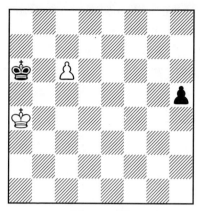

Diagram 30
White to move

At first glance, White's position is hopeless. He can't catch Black's pawn, and his own pawn could be easily stopped by the Black king. But as White's king moves to support his advanced pawn, Black must take the time to move his own king to defend against its promotion. Suddenly White's king is within the magic square, able to catch the opposing pawn and draw!

1. Kb4 Kb6

If 1. ... h4, then 2. Kc5 h3 3. Kd6 h2 4. c7 Kb7 5. Kd7 with the draw.

2. Kc4 h4 3. Kd5 h3

Or 3. ... Kc7 4. Ke4.

4. Kd6 h2 5. c7, draw.

HOW TO WIN A PAWN UP: THREE RULES FOR BATTLING A BLOCKING KING

Blocking the pawn, the best defense short of winning the pawn, doesn't always draw—unless the pawn is a rook's pawn. (We'll take a look at this special case in a moment.) The side with the pawn should keep in mind the three rules for winning.

1. Move your king in front of your pawn. (This means, given a choice, you will move your king before advancing your pawn.)

Diagram 31
A key position: With Black to move, White has the opposition and wins with all non-rook pawns. On move, White only draws.

Diagram 32
White or Black to move The king is not in front of his pawn—draw!

2. With your king in front (either directly or diagonally) of your pawn, you'll always win, except when the defender has the opposition. One king has the opposition when he stands in the path of his counterpart with one square between them on a file (most commonly), rank or diagonal—and his counterpart must move. This is frequently called the "direct" or "close opposition." It's important to keep in mind that the opposition is a tool to advance or to stop a pawn; opposition is not a goal in itself.

3. With your king on the sixth rank in front of your pawn, you'll always win, regardless of whose move it is. Memorize this next position. If you have the extra pawn, know that if you reach it there is no stopping you from winning. If you're the defender, you want to avoid this "and wins" position! It also illustrates the basic process of supporting the pawn while forcing the defender from the queening square.

Diagram 33

Here, White wins regardless of who's on move.

1. Ka6!

Because the extra pawn is a knight's pawn (b- or g-pawn), White needs to be careful not to box Black into a stalemate. In the case of 1. Kc6 Ka7 2. Kc7 (2. b6+ Ka8 leads only to a draw) 2. ... Ka8 3. b6?, it's a stalemate, but White wins repeating the position with 3. Kb6, then going to the right plan. This stalemate trap works only with knight-pawns, but with these, it works often. Remember it—especially when defending!

1. ... Ka8

Or 1. ... Kc8 2. Ka7.

2. b6 Kb8 3. b7

Hitting the seventh *without check*—a bad omen for the defender!

3. ... Kc7 4. Ka7

MOVE YOUR KING IN *FRONT* OF YOUR NON-ROOK PAWN, AND YOU'LL WIN UNLESS YOUR OPPONENT HAS THE OPPOSITION. WITH YOUR KING ON ITS *SIXTH* RANK IN *FRONT* OF YOUR PAWN, YOU'LL *ALWAYS* WIN!

Diagram 34

And the pawn queens.

Memorizing a few key, "matrix" positions is a tremendous help in calculating the result of trade-down combinations. Here's a classic illustration, the finale of a speed-game between Jose Capablanca and Emmanuel Lasker. Because Capa knew that he would win with his king on the sixth ahead of his pawn, that's as far as he needed to look. See Diagram 38 on page 42.

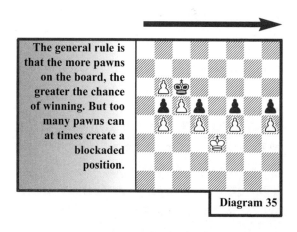

The general rule is that the more pawns on the board, the greater the chance of winning. But too many pawns can at times create a blockaded position.

Diagram 35

Most Winnable Endgames— the more pawns, the more winnable!

Diagram 36

No matter who moves, it's an easy draw.

Diagram 37

White creates an outside passed pawn and wins.

*Easiest win: Pawn endings **Next-easiest win:** Knight and pawn*

PAWN ENDINGS—THE MORE PAWNS, THE GREATER THE WINNING CHANCES

K+1 vs. K   about 50% chance of winning
K+2 vs. K+1   about 90% chance of winning
K+3 vs. K+2   about 95% chance of winning
The more pawns, the greater the winning chances!

However, with many pawns, beware of blocked positions—see Diagram 35 at left.

IN-BETWEEN ENDGAMES

Bishops of same color, bishop vs. knight, and queen vs. queen.

LEAST WINNABLE ENDGAMES

Bishops of opposite color—with an extra pawn, only about 10% are winnable; even with two extra pawns, about 30-40% are still a draw. The second least winnable endings are rook endings.

ENDGAME PRINCIPLES ARE DIFFERENT!

IN THE OPENING AND MIDDLEGAME, WE WOULD NEARLY ALWAYS WANT AN EXTRA MOVE. IN THE ENDGAME, AS WE'VE SEEN, LOSING A MOVE IS SOMETIMES THE KEY TO WINNING! LIKEWISE, IN THE ENDGAME RUSHING TO ADVANCE A PAWN CAN BE A SERIOUS MISTAKE.

KEEP YOUR ELECTIVE PAWN MOVES IN RESERVE. IN MANY CASES, THESE OPTIONAL MOVES WILL ALLOW YOU TO TAKE THE OPPOSITION AND PUT YOUR OPPONENT IN ZUGZWANG.

CAPABLANCA—EM. LASKER

Diagram 38
White to move

After 1. Kc6 Nxb5, a draw seems inevitable. But Capablanca finds a way to win, with one of those sudden reductions to an atomic chess position.

1. Rxa8+! Kxa8

(If 1. ... Nxa8, then 2. Kc8 Nc7 3. Kxc7, winning. And after 1. ... Kb7, 2. Ra7+ is decisive.)

2. Kxc7 Ka7 3. Kc6

Winning the pawn—and reaching number 3 of "How to Win a Pawn Up," above.

Let's look at a position where the king and pawn are both on the sixth rank.

IF THE PAWN HITS ITS SEVENTH WITH CHECK—IT'S A DRAW. IF IT ISN'T CHECK—IT'S A WIN.

Diagram 39
White to move

1. d7+

When the pawn hits the beachhead of the seventh rank with check, it portends the draw.

1. ... Kd8 2. Kd6

Diagram 40

It's a stalemate. But what if, in the starting position, it were Black's move?

*Fact: Jose Capablanca was never
checkmated in tournament play.*

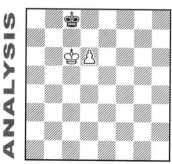

Diagram 41
Black to move

If it's Black's move, the pawn will advance without check, and White wins:

1. ... Kd8 2. d7 Ke7 3. Kc7.

With the White king unable to get ahead of his pawn, it's a draw—but the defender has to play accurately.

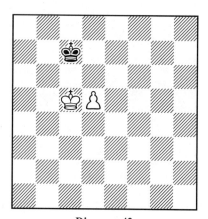

Diagram 42

1. d6+ Kd7 2. Kd5

Diagram 43

If Black's king falls back to c8 or e8, he's doomed, because he invites a pawn advance that doesn't give check. For example, after 2. ... Kc8 3. Kc6 Kd8 4. d7, the pawn advances without checking, Black's king is chased off the queening square, and White promotes and wins. And after 2. ... Ke8, 3. Ke6 (or 3. Kc6) wins in the same manner. Black must drop straight back to keep the draw.

2. ... Kd8

Now Black can, after 3. Ke6, respond with 3. .... Ke8, and on 3. Kc6, play ... Kc8. He thus keeps the opposition, not giving White's pawn a chance to advance without check, and draws. And, of course, Black meets the tricky 3. Ke5 with 3. ... Kd7, returning to his safest square.

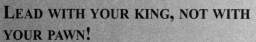

LEAD WITH YOUR KING, NOT WITH YOUR PAWN!

ROOK PAWNS — WHEN LIVING ON THE EDGE CAN BE SAFE

When the extra pawn is a rook pawn, the odds of a win plummet, since the possibility of stalemate protects the defender from normal winning techniques. If the defender's king can simply get to the queening square, he can't be forced out regardless of who has the opposition.

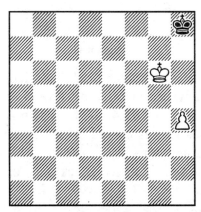

Diagram 44
Black to move

This is a draw because White can't budge the opponent's king from the corner. Pushing the pawn to h7 leads to stalemate.

DEFENDING BY JAILING THE OPPOSING KING ON THE ROOK'S FILE

Even if the opposing king is in the otherwise ideal position—on the sixth rank ahead of his pawn, the game can often be drawn.

Diagram 45
White to move

This is a draw, regardless of who is on move. A blockade is successful thanks to Black's access to the c7 and c8 squares.

For example:

1. Ka7 Kc7 2. a6 Kc8 3. Kb6 Kb8

Or with Black on move:

1. ... Kc7 2. Ka7

If 2. Kb5, 2. ... Kb7.

2. ... Kc8 3. a6 Kc7 4. Ka8 Kc8 5. a7 Kc7 stalemate.

Diagram 46

You can see that even if the superior side's king actually occupies the queening square, as long as the defender can get to the seventh or eighth rank of the bishop's file, it's a dead draw.

Even extra rook pawns don't help the superior side.

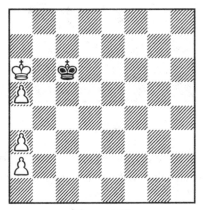

Diagram 47
White or Black to move

Black draws easily. He keeps White's king a prisoner on the rook's file or, if the White king escapes, Black heads for the corner, from which he can't be pried.

Once again, knowing this simple rule makes it possible to stop calculations upon arriving at similar positions. In one of his

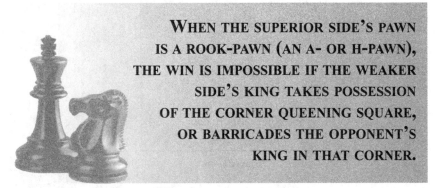

WHEN THE SUPERIOR SIDE'S PAWN
IS A ROOK-PAWN (AN A- OR H-PAWN),
THE WIN IS IMPOSSIBLE IF THE WEAKER
SIDE'S KING TAKES POSSESSION
OF THE CORNER QUEENING SQUARE,
OR BARRICADES THE OPPONENT'S
KING IN THAT CORNER.

games, Mikhail Tal shows us how to use the rule to find the right way to a draw in a difficult and complicated position.

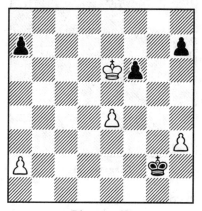

Diagram 48
Black to move

1. ... Kf3 2. Kxf6 Kxe4 3. h4 Kd5 4. h5 Kd6

Black is organizing a defense by trying to incarcerate his opponent's king on the edge of the board.

5. Kg7 Ke7 6. Kxh7 Kf7 7. h6 a5!

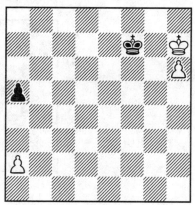

Diagram 49

8. a4 Kf8 9. Kg6 Kg8 10. Kf6 Kh7 11. Ke5 Kxh6
12. Kd5 Kg6 13. Kc5 Kf6 14. Kb5 Ke6 15. Kxa5 Kd7

Diagram 50

16. Kb6 Kc8

Black's king is just in time (17. Ka7 Kc7) to block his adversary. Moving the pawn to a5 was necessary to distract White's king from the key square of b7. If the pawn remained at home, or even moved only to a6, Black would lose: 7. ... a6 8. a4 Kf8? (8. ... a5! =) 9. Kg6 Kg8 10. a5 Kh8 11. Kf6 Kh7 12. Ke6 Kxh6 13. Kd6 Kg6 14. Kc6 Kf6 15. Kb7 Ke6 16. Kxa6 Kd7 17. Kb7.

Diagram 51
After 17. Kb7

Black loses because he wasn't able to get to the corner or limit White's king to the side of the board. Now that we've looked at the special case of the rook-pawn, let's move on to other principles.

SAFE SQUARES

When the defender can stand on a square and draw, that square is a "safe square." Take a careful look at the next diagram, which so far has no defending king. Where could we put the Black king so that it can draw? How many such *safe squares* are there?

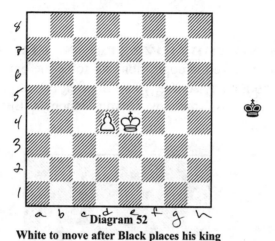

Diagram 52
White to move after Black places his king

Well, e6 and d6 should be pretty obvious to you by now. If on e6, the Black King has only one good square to move to—d6. And, conversely, if he's on d6, then e6 is the only safe square.

Reminder—never move to the side! Here 1. ... Kc6? and 1. ... Kf6? both lose miserably. And never, ever voluntarily move backward: 1. ... Ke7? loses to 2. Ke5, grabbing the opposition after 2. ... Kd7 3. Kd5. *Taking the opposition when ahead of the pawn diagonally inevitably leads to having the opposition in front of the pawn.* With the White king on d5 and Black's king on d7, Black must move over and let White's king gain more space and secure the queening of the pawn. Similarly, 2. ... Kd7 loses to 2. Kd5.

So two other safe squares are d8 and e8. Here, Black is never in zugzwang, as he goes back and forth between these two squares. He meets 1. Kd5 with 1. ... Kd7, or 1. Ke5 with

1. ... Ke7, taking the opposition—thus preventing White's king from making any progress.

So Black draws with his king on (or moving to) any of *four* safe squares:

1. ... Ke6, 1. ... Kd6, 1. ... Ke8, or 1. ... Kd8.

PASSING THE MOVE (TRIANGULATION)

In order to take the opposition and force the opposing king to move from a key square, you will often need to find a way to effectively "pass" the move to your opponent. But how can you "pass"?

NEDELKOVICH

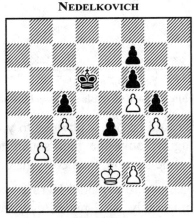

Diagram 53
White to move

The immediate fight is for the e4 pawn. White can't win it immediately after 1. Ke3 Ke5, but he can triangulate on the e2-d2-e3 squares to "lose" a move, forcing Black into a zugzwang.

1. Kd2 Ke5 2. Ke3, winning.

The e-pawn is lost. White would then create a passed pawn on the queenside by moving his king to c3 and playing b3-b4.

CALLING IN THE RESERVES

In the fight for opposition, extra moves available to the pawns can be crucial. Such moves can be used to force the opponent into zugzwang.

Diagram 54
White to move

If White's pawn were already on d4, White, to move, wouldn't be able to win because Black would keep the opposition.

1. d4

This move forces Black to give way for the opposing monarch.

1. ... Kc7 2. Ke6, winning.

Similarly, 1. ... Ke7 2. Kc6, leads to a win for White.

WHEN THERE ARE A COUPLE OF PAWNS ON THE BOARD, TRIANGULATING CAN BE THE RIGHT TOOL, "HANDING BACK" A POSITION TO YOUR OPPONENT.

FILIP—BARCZA
SOFIA, 1957

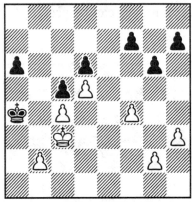

Diagram 55
White to move

In this complex position, Black plans to provoke b2-b3+, which
would allow his king to penetrate into the opponent's camp. It
is important that after both sides exhaust the pawn moves on the
king side, Black will have a reserve pawn move, … a6-a5, on
the opposite side of the board.

1. g3

If 1. g4 h5 2. gxh5 gxh5 3. f5 f6 4. h4 a5!, and 5. b3+ is forced.

1. … f5 2. g4 h5 3. gxh5 gxh5 4. h4 a5.

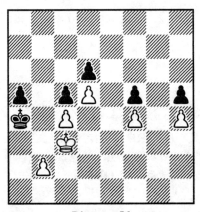

Diagram 56

5. b3+

If 5. Kc2, then 5. ... Kb4 6. b3 a4 7. bxa4.

Diagram 57
After 7. bxa4

7. ... Kxa4 (7. ... Kxc4 also wins) 8. Kc3 Ka3 9. Kc2 Kb4 10. Kd3 Kb3, with the win.

5. ... Ka3 6. Kc2 Ka2

Black also wins with 6. ... a4, as in Diagram 57.

7. Kc3

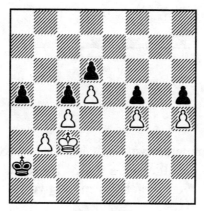

Diagram 58
Black to move

7. ... Kb1

This important maneuver from behind wins.

8. Kd3 Kb2 9. Kd2 Kxb3, White resigns.

THE MOVING SCREEN

The next technique we'll take a look at is the chess king's equivalent of the "moving screen," sometimes called a "moving pick"—a tactic illegal in basketball but permitted in chess. Trainers in Russia call this "shoulder-pushing." This most effective tool yields several advantages at once. One king moves across the board in a way that gives him the shortest route to a pawn or pawns while simultaneously preventing the rival king from following the shortest route to his objective.

SHADE—AHUES
BERLIN, 1921

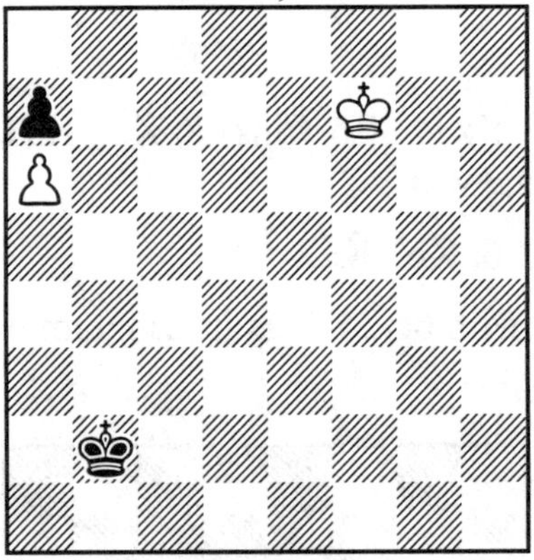

Diagram 59
White to move

1. Ke6 Kc3

Now White blundered with 2. Kd6? Kd4 3. Kc6 Ke5 4. Kb7 Kd6 5. Kxa7 Kc7, allowing a draw. By screening (or "shoulder-pushing," if you prefer) on move two, White could have won.

2. Kd5

White's goal is Black's pawn on a7; Black's goal is the safe haven of the c7-square.

Diagram 60

White's king approaches the a7-pawn while at the same time shouldering his opponent's king away from c7. Now 2. ... Kb4 is as hopeless as the text move.

> **2. ... Kd3 3. Kc6 Kd4 4. Kb7 Kc5 5. Kxa7 Kc6 6. Kb8, winning.**

Diagram 61

THE "MOVING SCREEN" ACCOMPLISHES TWO GOALS AT ONCE: USING THE SHORTEST ROUTE TO HIS GOAL AND PREVENTING THE ENEMY KING FROM DOING THE SAME.

THE DISTANT OPPOSITION

You've seen how important the *direct* or close opposition can be, often making the difference between a win and a draw. When the kings are distant from each other, it's crucial to recognize how you can wind up with the direct opposition.

CAPABLANCA

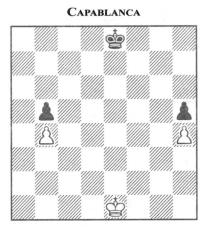

Diagram 62
White to move

1. Ke2!

Taking the *distant* opposition, since there are now an odd number (5) of squares between the kings, and it's Black to move. If both kings advanced straight ahead, White would wind up with the close opposition.

1. ... Ke7

On 1. ... Kd8, White sidesteps with 2. Kf3. After 2. ... Ke7, White continues 3. Ke3! (another distant opposition, with three squares between the kings) 3. ... Kf7 4. Kd4 (sidestepping again to gain the opposition) 4. ... Kf6 5. Kc5, winning. After 1. ... Kf8, Black also loses: 2. Kd3 Ke7 3. Ke3! Kd7 4. Kf4. If 1. ... Kf7, then 2. Kf3 Ke7 3. Ke3! +-.

2. Ke3! Ke6

If 2. ... Kf6, then 3. Kf4.

3. Ke4

Diagram 63

3. ... Kf6

Now some calculations are needed. If 3. ... Kd6 4. Kd4! Kc6 (4. ... Ke6 5. Kc5, and White queens well ahead of Black.) 5. Ke5 Kb6 6. Kd6 Kb7 7. Kc5 Ka6 8. Kc6 Ka7 9. Kxb5 Kb7 10. Kc5 Kc7 11. Kd5 Kb6 12. Ke5 Kb5 13. Kf5 Kxb4 14. Kg5 +-

Diagram 64
After 14. Kg5

4. Kf4

Running immediately for the b-pawn with 4. Kd5? would be a mistake, leading to a draw after 4. ... Kf5.

4. ... Kg6

If 4. ... Ke6, White wins with 5. Kg5.

5. Ke5 Kf7 6. Kf5 Kg7 7. Kg5 Kf7 8. Kxh5 Kf6 9. Kg4 Kg6 10. Kf4, winning.

Here's a beautiful and practical illustration of both safe squares and the power of the opposition. Of course, if it's Black's move, he wins easily with 1. ... Kd4. But, with the move, can White save the draw? Remember, you definitely don't want Black to win the White pawn in a way that leaves his king in front of his own pawn with either the opposition or a reserve pawn move.

Diagram 65
White to move

With all this in mind, you can find ...

1. e5! dxe5 2. Kc1!

Not 2. Kc2? Kc4! -+.

2. ... Kd5

If 2. ... Kd4, then 3. Kd2; if 2. ... Kc4, then 3. Kc2.

3. Kd1

White draws because he reaches his safe squares, d1 and e1.

UNLIKE REAL LIFE, STEPPING ASIDE
DIAGONALLY IS AS "SHORT" A PATH
AS TRAVELING STRAIGHT AHEAD
ON THE RANK OR FILE.

NEISHTADT

Diagram 66
White to move

White achieves a draw in this seemingly hopeless position by using the distant opposition.

1. Kh1!!

With this position in mind, William Blake could have written "What immortal hand or eye/Could frame thy *draw*ful symmetry?" 1. Kf1 is bad because of 1. ... Kd2 2. Kf2 g4! (the "waiting" move 2. ... Kd3 also wins) 3. fxg4 e4 4. g5 e3+. Also losing is 1. Kg3 Ke1 2. Kg2 Ke2 3. Kg3 Kf1! 4. Kg4 Kf2 -+.

1. ... Ke2

If 1. ... g4, then 2. Kg2!, with a draw.

2. Kg2 Ke3 3. Kg3 Kd4 4. Kg4 Ke3 5. Kg3 Ke2 6. Kg2 Kd2 7. Kh2!

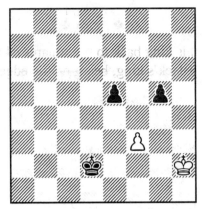

Diagram 67

Maintaining the balance, thanks to the distant opposition.

7. ... Kd3 8. Kh3!, draw.

THE CLASSIC TRIANGULATION

Now it pays to take a look back at passing the move in close quarters. You'll want to memorize this example.

Diagram 68
White to move

1. Kd5 Kc8!

Now the straightforward 2. Kd6 doesn't work because 2. ... Kd8

3. c7+ leads only to stalemate. But if, in the position after 1. ... Kc8, Black had to move, he would lose. Time for White to pass! He moves his king back to the squares c4 and d4 in order to lose a tempo. Black's king, being on the edge, doesn't enjoy such an option.

2. Kc4 Kd8

Or 2. ... Kb8 brings us to the same end.

3. Kd4 Kc8

If 3. ... Kc7 4. Kc5.

4. Kd5

The move's been passed! We're back to the position after Black's 1. ... Kc8, only now it's Black's turn.

Diagram 69

Now Black loses after 4. ... Kc7 5. Kc5 Kc8 6. Kb6, or 4. ... Kd8 5. Kd6 Kc8 6. c7 Kb7 7. Kd7.

PART II: PASSED PAWNS

Let's now focus on those positions, with several pawns on the board, where the passed pawns are a decisive factor. A passed pawn is one that isn't blocked by another pawn and doesn't have enemy pawns on adjoining files. In other words, no pawns can stop it on its march to promotion. In a king-and-pawn ending, a passed pawn can be stopped only by the opponent's king. Since the opposing king must be at all times able to prevent a passed pawn from queening, it's important to be able to tell how close to the pawn he must stay.

THE ADVANTAGE OF THE OUTSIDE PASSED PAWNS

CHEKHOVER

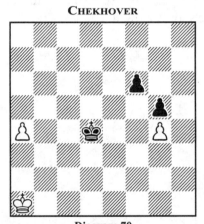

Diagram 70
White to move

Black's king has to catch White's passed a-pawn. For his part, White plans to take his opponent's pawns on the kingside and then to win the game by promoting his g-pawn. Black's attempt to create counterplay fails.

1. a5 Kc5

If Black tries 1. ... Kd5, play continues 2. Kb2 f5 3. gxf5 g4 4. a6 Kc6 5. f6 g3 6. a7 Kb7 7. f7 g2.

Diagram 71
After 7. ... g2

8. a8(Q+)!—an important, tempo-winning technique—8. ...
Kxa8 9. f8(Q+), winning. Back to the main line.

2. Kb2 f5

The only try for counterplay. In the case of 2. ... Kb5 3. Kc3
Kxa5 4. Kd4 Kb6 5. Ke4 (5. Kd5? f5 6. gxf5 g4 7. Ke4 Kc6=)
5. ... Kc7 6. Kf5 Kd7 7. Kxf6 Ke8 8. Kxg5 Kf7 9. Kh6, White
is winning.

3. gxf5 g4 4. f6 Kd6 5. a6 g3 6. f7 Ke7 7. a7 g2 8.
f8(Q)+, winning.

It is important to note the distracting roles played by the a- and
f-pawns.

THE MAIN TASK OF THE DISTANT PASSED
PAWN IS TO DISTRACT THE OPPONENT'S
KING, WHILE ON THE OTHER SIDE OF
THE BOARD ITS OWN KING ATTACKS
DEFENSELESS PAWNS BEREFT OF THEIR
KING'S SUPPORT.

Here's a position with much more than kings and pawns, so it looks a little out of place in this chapter. But it again illustrates how such a complex position can reduce itself to the chess "atom" we began this chapter by discussing. And it shows the distracting power of a distant passed pawn.

LOMBARDY—FISCHER
NEW YORK, 1960

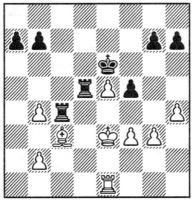

Diagram 72
Black to move

Black sacrifices the Exchange in order to segue into a favorable pawn ending, where he can count on a distant, outside passed pawn.

1. ... Rxc3+ 2. bxc3 Rxe5+ 3. Kd2 Rxe1 4. Kxe1 Kd5 5. Kd2 Kc4 6. h5 b6!

Black prepares ... a7-a5.

PASSED PAWNS ARE MEANT TO DISTRACT! AND THE FARTHER THE OPPONENT'S KING IS FROM THE PASSED PAWN, THE STRONGER ITS POWER TO DISTRACT.

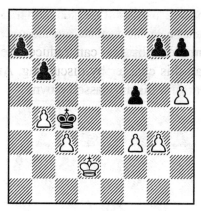

Diagram 73

7. Kc2 g5 8. h6 f4!

This is an important moment. Black advances his kingside-passed pawns as far he can. After the upcoming exchanges on the queenside, he wants his f-pawn as close to its promotion square as possible.

9. g4 a5 10. bxa5 bxa5 11. Kb2 a4 12. Ka3 Kxc3

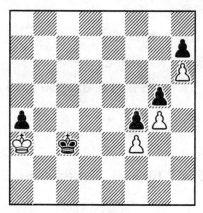

Diagram 74

13. Kxa4 Kd4 14. Kb4 Ke3, and White resigns.

Although important, a distant passed pawn does not always guarantee advantage. A lot depends on the overall pawn structure and position of the kings.

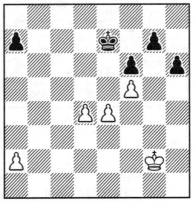

EUWE—SPIELMAN
AMSTERDAM, 1930

Diagram 75
White to move

Black's kingside pawns are not favorably placed. Here Black's distant passed h-pawn is no match for White's far-advanced, powerful central passers.

1. Kg3 Kf7 2. Kh4 Ke7

Or 2. ... g6 3. fxg6+ Kxg6 4. d5 Kg7 5. Kh5 +-.

3. Kh5 Kf7 4. e5 fxe5 5. dxe5 a6 6. a3 a5 7. a4 Kf8 8. Kg6 h5

If Black tries 8. ... Kg8, there follows 9. e6 Kf8 10. e7+, winning.

9. Kxh5 Kf7 10. Kg5, Black resigns.

MUTUAL DEFENSE TREATIES
BETWEEN PAWNS

Two passed pawns, either of which by themselves would be vulnerable to capture by the enemy king, in effect often defend each other. Capturing one would put the king out of reach to stop the other from running to its promotion square.

Diagram 76
White to move

Here there are two White pawns, one file apart. They "protect" each other because if Black's king stops to capture one, its partner reaches escape velocity toward the queening square.

1. d4! Kd5 2. b5 Kd6

So endings, as well as openings, can have "poison" pawns!

3. Kg2 Kc7

The threat is 4. ... Kb6.

4. d5! Kb6 5. d6 Kb7 6. Kg3 Kb6 7. Kxg4, winning.

The idea of pawns supporting each other is well expressed in the following position.

PROKEC

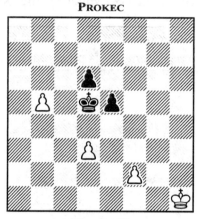

Diagram 77
White to move

1. f4 exf4

If Black tries 1. ... Kc5, White plays 2. f5, winning.

2. d4

Ingenious—and perfectly logical, based on what you've already seen. Black can't capture the pawn on d4 because he would put himself outside of the Berger Square of the b-pawn and be unable to stop it from queening. And the d4-pawn keeps the Black king from using c5. He has to try a long walk through a side door, giving White's king the time he needs to win the Black pawns.

2. ... Ke6 3. Kg2 Kd7 4. Kf3 Kc7 5. Kxf4 Kb6 6. Ke4 Kxb5 7. Kd5, winning.

Connected passed pawns can protect each other in much the same way.

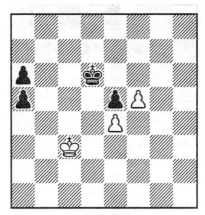

Diagram 78
White to move

White's pawns are unapproachable, while Black's pawns, separated and weak, are easy prey. White wins easily by capturing the a-pawns, and then coming back for the e5-pawn.

Max Euwe (1901-1981), the fifth official world champion, and the only "amateur" champion since Paul Morphy.

Courtesy USCF

PROKEC

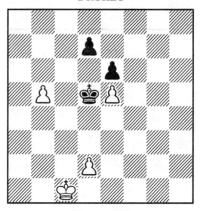

Diagram 79
White to move

Watch how White uses various techniques allowing the pawns to protect each other.

1. d4 d6 2. b6

If 2. exd6?, then ... Kxd6 3. Kc2 e5 4. dxe5+ Kxe5 5. Kb3 Kd6, draw.

2. ... Kc6

Now an unexpected breakthrough proves decisive.

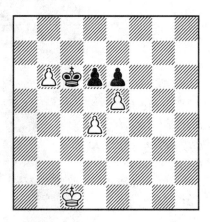

Diagram 80

3. d5+!

Diagram 81

3. ... Kxb6

After 3. ... exd5, White wins with 4. e6.

4. dxe6 Kc7 5. e7 Kd7 6. exd6, winning.

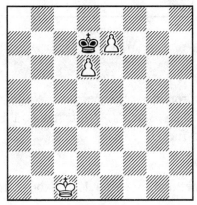

Diagram 82

CREATING PASSED PAWNS—RADICAL BREAKTHROUGHS

The most radical technique in the pawn ending is the breakthrough. Breakthroughs create passed pawns almost out of thin air. But one side's pawns have to be far enough advanced so he can throw them at their blocking opponents in a kamikaze fashion that forces a passed pawn near a promotion square. In all cases, the breakthrough requires the sacrifice of one or even a couple of pawns, as well as the absence of the enemy king from the resulting Berger Square. The following example is classic.

Diagram 83
White to move

1. b6!

Here the breakthrough works because White's pawns are far more advanced than Black's. White takes a Black pawn off either the a- or c-file.

1. ... cxb6

There is a symmetrical line after 1. ... axb6 2. c6 bxc6 3. a6.

2. a6

This move dislodges the b7 pawn.

2. ... bxa6 3. c6

And the c-pawn has a clear path to promotion because the Black king is too far away to stop it. With the move, Black could have defended with 1. ... b6! (not 1. ... a6 2. c6!, or 1. ... c6 2. a6!; in case of 1. ... Kg6, the king is still too distant, and 2. b6 wins), preventing the breakthrough. Were Black's king on g6, then he would actually have won with 1. ... Kf5.

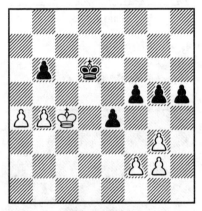

Diagram 84
Black to move

In this position, Black played 1. ... h4? and lost. But Black should create a passed pawn on the kingside and *win* with ...

1. ... f4! 2. gxf4

If 2. a5, then 2. ... bxa5 3. bxa5 h4, with the threat of ... f4-f3 and promotion of the h-pawn.

2. ... gxf4 3. Kd4 e3 4. fxe3

On 4. Kd3, Black uncorks 4. ... f3!. There follows 5. gxf3 h4 6. Ke2 h3 7. Kf1 e2+.

4. ... f3!!

Diagram 85

5. gxf3 h4, winning.

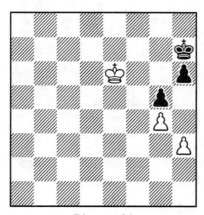

Diagram 86
White to move

Here the dominant position of the White king forces Black to push his h-pawn—otherwise, he loses both pawns!

1. Kf7 h5

Now if 2. Kf6, then 2. ... hxg4 3. hxg4 Kh6 4. Kf5 Kh7 5. Kxg5 Kg7, with a draw.

2. h4!

Diagram 87

2. ... Kh6

Or 2. ... gxh4 3.g5.

**3. Kf6 gxh4 4. g5+ Kh7 5. Kf7 h3 6. g6+ Kh6 7. g7 h2
8. g8(Q) h1(Q) 9. Qg6 mate.**

Just the Facts!

ED LASKER—MOLL
CHICAGO, 1912

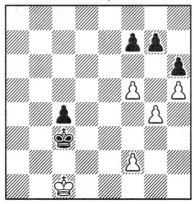

Diagram 88
White to move

At first glance, Black seems to have an "obvious" win. The c-
pawn will distract White's king, while all of the White pawns
on the other side will be taken. But there is a surprising opportunity for a winning White breakthrough.

1. f6!

White's 1. f4 loses to 1. ... f6!, which closes the kingside gate!
Then if 2. g5, Black doesn't capture—and White can't create a
passed pawn.

1. ... gxf6 2. f4 Kd4

Black rushes to catch up with White's potential passed pawn.

3. g5 fxg5 4. fxg5 Ke5 5. gxh6 Kf6 6. Kc2

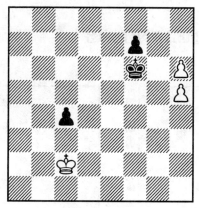

Diagram 89

6. ... c3 7. Kxc3, Black resigns.

Note how White's doubled rook pawns created a zugzwang, because Black is blocked by his own f7 pawn. Without it, he would retreat to h8 and draw easily.

Summary: You should be constantly alert to sudden transitions to an endgame, and what that would mean to your prospects. King position and the presence of passed pawns are the two most important features of pawn endings. As a defender, try to get in front (block) a passer with your king. If you have the extra pawn, advance your king ahead of your pawn. The Rule of the Square will help you tell quickly if an unsupported pawn can queen. Memorizing a few key "matrix" positions will provide a shortcut to evaluating positions. The chances of winning plummet when the sole extra pawn is a rook-pawn.

The concepts of safe squares, triangulation, reserve pawn moves, the "moving screen," and opposition are important to playing these endings well.

The outside passed pawn frequently wins because it can be used to distract the defense. Passed pawns and connected passed pawns can protect each other. Passed pawns can be created by the breakthrough technique.

Pawn Ending
Learning Exercises

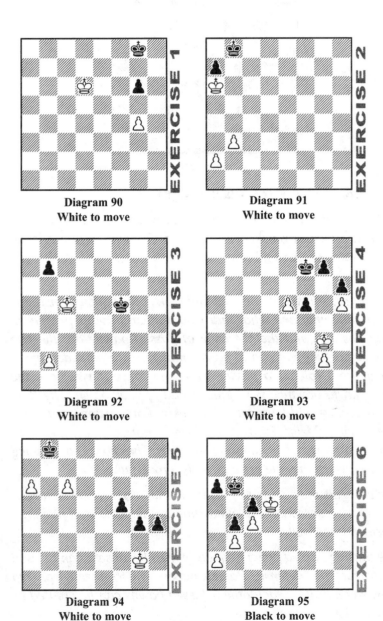

Diagram 90
White to move

Diagram 91
White to move

Diagram 92
White to move

Diagram 93
White to move

Diagram 94
White to move

Diagram 95
Black to move

Pawn Endings
Solutions

Diagram 96
White to move

Diagram 97
White to move

No. 1 **1. g5! Kf7 2. Kd7 Kf8 3. Ke6 Kg7 4. Ke7 Kg8 5. Kf6 Kh7 6. Kf7 Kh8 7. Kxg6 Kg8 8. Kh6 Kh8 9. g6 Kg8 10. g7 Kf7 11. Kh7 +-.**

No. 2 **1. b4 Ka8 2. b5 Kb8 3. a3! Ka8 4. a4 Kb8 5. a5 Ka8 6. b6 axb6 7. axb6 Kb8 8. b7 +-.** (With Black to move, White wins by playing a2-a4 in one move!)

No. 3 **1. Kd5!** (1. Kb6 Ke5 2. b4 Kd5 3. b5 Kc4=; 1. b4 Ke6 2. Kb6 Kd5=) **1. ... Kf6 2. Kd6 Kf5 3. b4 Ke4 4. b5 Kd4 5. b6 Kc4 6. Kc7 Kb5 7. Kxb7 +-.**

No. 4 **1. Kf3!** (1. Kf4? g6 2. hxg6+ Kxg6 3. g3 h5 4. e6 Kf6 5. e7 Kxe7 6. Kxf5 h4 =) **1. ... g6** (1. ... Ke7 2. Kf4 Ke6 3. g3 +-) **2. hxg6+ Kxg6 3. Kf4 h5 4. g3 +-** (zugzwang).

No. 5 **1. Kh2 f4** (1. ... g3+ 2. Kh3 f4 3. Kg2 +-) **2. Kg1! h3** (2. ... g3 3. Kg2 +-) **3. Kh2 f3 4. Kg3 h2 5. Kxh2 f2 6. Kg2 g3 7. Kf1 +-** (zugzwang).

No. 6 **1. ... Ka5 2. Kxc5 stalemate.**

No. 7 **1. b5 Kg4 2. c5 Kf5 3. b6 cxb6 4. c6 bxc6 5. axb6+- or 2. ... dxc5 3. b6 cxb6 4. d6 +-, or 2. ... axb5 3. c6 bxc6 4. a6 +-.**

No. 8 **1. c6! bxc6 2. b4 axb4 3. Kd4 +-.**

Chapter 3: Pawns against Pieces
Some Important Ideas to Look For

◆When a knight on the rim isn't dim

Whoever moves, Black's lone knight prevents the pawn from promoting.
See Diagram 101.

◆Restraining two pawns at once

Black plays 1. ... Bd6.
See Diagram 132.

◆The cut-off play

White plays 1. Rg5, winning easily.
See Diagram 141.

◆Refuge in the corner

Black plays 4. ... Ka1.
See Diagram 162.

Chapter 3
Pawns against Pieces:
Running the Gauntlet

The meek *can* inherit the earth. Endgames are most often won or lost because a pawn, the lowliest foot soldier, has survived the earlier stages of battle and makes the dangerous but rewarding march to the other end of the board. If he reaches his goal, he's promoted to the status of his commander's choice. Of course, whatever resources his enemy has left are concentrated on stopping this little social climber.

In this chapter, to emphasize the pattern of thinking you'll want to emulate in your own, real games, we'll organize around a "plan-and-play" approach.

PAWN VERSUS KNIGHT
Pawns with the "lust to expand" create the most troubles for the slow-moving knight. The a- and h- passed pawns are particu-

larly dangerous for the knight because the horseman's moves
are restricted at the edge of the board. Let's look at the positions
where the knight is opposed by a single pawn.

ZEPLER

Diagram 98
White or Black to move

Here it's obvious that White must preserve his pawn if he hopes
to win. Conversely, if Black has a chance to capture the ambi-
tious pawn, he does so immediately, with disregard for the fate
of his knight, since the game is then instantly drawn.

THE PLAN
White will advance his king to c6. The knight will have to
retreat to the corner. Then White's king captures the horseman
by moving to b7. If Black is not able to bring his king to c7 in
time to stalemate the White king, Black loses.

THE PLAY
The first question for the White king is how to get to c6. Black's
knight creates roadblocks in two ways. Of course, the squares it
covers are off limits to the White king. But in addition, the king
must be careful not to step on those special, landmine-squares
that trigger a knight check which forks king and pawn! These
mined squares are d4 and d6, because of the knight check on b5.
The invading king can choose between only two circuitous but

safe side paths. One is through d3, c4 and c5 and the other—through e5, f6, e7, d7.

This last way is one move too slow:

1. Ke5 Kg2 2. Kf6 Kf3 3. Ke7 Ke4 4. Kd7 Na8 5. Kc6 Ke5 6. Kb7 Kd6 7. Kxa8 Kc7.

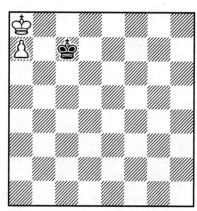

Diagram 99
White to move

The Black king reaches his key square in time, stalemating.

But taking the "low road," in this case, gives White a win. From Diagram 98:

1. Kd3! Kg2 2. Kc4 Kf3 3. Kc5 Ke4 4. Kc6 Na8 5. Kb7 Kd5 6. Kxa8 Kc6 7. Kb8

The move is there,
but you must see it!
      —Tartakover

Diagram 100

And the White pawn queens.

WHEN THE LONE HORSEMAN HOLDS OFF BOTH KING AND ROOK PAWN

Now we come to an example of a very interesting and useful rule.

Diagram 101
White to move

There's no way for White's king to drive away the knight. It doesn't make any difference whose move it is. If it's Black to move, he advances his king, or for that matter, simply shuffles it back and forth, since the knight holds on its own—but you need to know the technique. With White to move ...

1. Kb6 Nc8+ 2. Kb7 Nd6+ 3. Kc7 Nb5+ 4. Kb6 Nd6!, and Black holds.

Ready to answer 5. a7 with 5. ... Nc8+, forking king and pawn.

IF THE DEFENDING KNIGHT OCCUPIES THE SQUARE DIRECTLY IN FRONT OF AN ENEMY ROOK PAWN THAT IS ON ITS SIXTH RANK, THEN THE GAME IS A DRAW, NO MATTER HOW FAVORABLY PLACED THE ENEMY KING OR HOW DISTANT THE DEFENDER'S KING.

SOZIN

Diagram 102
White to move

THE PLAN

Knowing the knight's ability to be the sole savior if it's allowed to occupy the key spot on a7, White tries to cut off the knight from the pawn's path to glory, while advancing the would-be queen.

THE PLAY

1. Kc5!

Restricting the knight. If 1. a6, then 1. ... Nd6+ 2. Kb6 Kf2 would lead to a draw.

1. ... Ne5

If 1. ... Nd8, then 2. a6 Ne6+ 3. Kb6 +-.

2. a6 Nd7+ 3. Kb5 Nf8 4. a7 Ne6 5. Kb6, winning.

YOU CAN'T *ALWAYS* WIN

Even with best play, it's not always possible to execute the winning plan, to push a knight away and prevent the approach of the opponent's king.

Diagram 103
White or Black to play

The great German grandmaster and teacher Siegbert Tarrasch, warned "Der Springer am Rande ist immer Schande!" A knight on the edge (of the board) is always a shame. To follow his rhyming spirit, we often translate his remark to "A knight on the rim is dim." The knight can't stop a *rook*-pawn on its seventh, but it can often stop other pawns.

THE PLAY

1. Kf7

If 1. Kh7 Ne7!; or even 1. ... Nf6+.

1. ... Nh6+ 2. Kf6 Ke3 3. Kg6 Ng8 4. Kh7 Ne7, draw.

WHEN THE KNIGHT IS IN FRONT OF A *NON*-ROOK PAWN THAT IS ON ITS SEVENTH RANK, THE LONE KNIGHT CAN HOLD THE DRAW, WITHOUT HIS KING'S HELP!

Diagram 104
Black to move

Even with Black to move, White is winning.

> **1. ... Ne7+**

Or 1. ... Nf6+ 2. Kf7 Ng4 3. Kg6 Ne5+ 4. Kg5 Nf7+ 5. Kh5.

> **2. Kf8! Ng6+ 3. Ke8, Black resigns.**

WHEN THE KNIGHT IS *NOT* IN FRONT OF THE PAWN
ON THE SEVENTH RANK, THE DEFENSE IS MORE
DIFFICULT. IN THE CASE OF THE KNIGHT PAWN,
THE DEFENSE IS ESPECIALLY DIFFICULT,
BECAUSE IT FORCES THE KNIGHT TO BE
"DIM ON THE RIM." BISHOP AND CENTER
PAWNS ARE EASIER TO DEFEND AGAINST,
BECAUSE THE KNIGHT CAN PLAY
ON BOTH SIDES OF THE BOARD.

Executive Editor
Al Lawrence

Former USCF Executive Director

Author of seven books on diverse topics

◆ *World Book Encyclopedia* contributor

◆ Former college and public school teacher

◆ Holder of advanced degrees in instructional techniques

◆ President of OutExcel! Corp.

◆ CEO of StarFinder, Inc.

◆ Consulting partner in www.ChessCafe.com

Place of Birth: Blue Island, Illinois
Date of Birth: February 5, 1947

Author and co-author of seven books on a variety of subjects, Al Lawrence edited and designed *Just the Facts!* with the goal of making it a pleasure to get the most out of the uniquely instructive ideas of GMs Alburt and Krogius. And to help you and your students win more games!

Lawrence was Executive Director of the U.S. Chess Federation during a decade of innovation and record-breaking growth. A former public school and college teacher with advanced degrees in instructional techniques, he is especially interested in applying modern teaching theory to chess.

He is president of OutExcel! Corporation, a marketing and publishing firm. He is also Chief Executive Officer of StarFinder, Inc., which develops and patents products that make it easy for amateur stargazers to enjoy observing the night sky. StarFinder's "Night Navigator" has been featured internationally in magazines and on television.

Lawrence is a consulting partner in one of the most popular chess websites—www.chesscafe.com. Chesscafe offers book reviews, photos, chess want ads, and articles by leading chess thinkers from around the world.

Diagram 105
Black to move

Black draws with …

> **1. ... Nd7+!**

If Black tries 1. ... Ne6+?, there follows 2. Ke7 Nf4 3. Kf6 Nd5+ 4. Kf5 Ne7+ 5. Kg5 +-.

> **2. Ke8**

Or 2. Ke7 Ne5 3. f8(Q) Ng6+.

> **2. ... Nf6+ 3. Ke7 Nh7, draw.**

In many positions, a knight survives the joust against a passed pawn, thanks to checks that allow the horseman to get to squares nearest the foot soldier.

GRIGORIEV

Diagram 106
White to move

THE PLAN

White's king is far away, so only the knight can stop the pawn. By the time the pawn is on b2, the knight must be able to hold b1. So the cavalryman must get to one of three squares: a3, c3, or d2, and then, happily, to a safe haven—b1. At first this task seems impossible. But White hops backward to go forward!

THE PLAY

1. Nc7+ Kc4

The strongest. If 1. ... Kd4, then 2. Kg2 b3 3. Nb5+ and 4. Na3 or 1. ... Kc6 2. Ne6 Kb5 3. Nd4+ Kc4 4. Nc6 b3 5. Na5+.

2. Ne8!

Again, a bit paradoxical, but best. The knight is moving away for the moment in order to start a pawn chase from d6 or f6 (depending on the White king's position). Now after 2. ... b3, there could follow 3. Nd6+ Kb4 4. Ne4 b2 5. Nd2. That's why Black's king next takes the d6-square under control.

2. ... Kc5 3. Nf6! Kd4 4. Ne8 Ke5

If 4. ... b3, then 5. Nd6 Kc3 6. Ne4+ Kc2 7. Nd6 b2 8. Nc4 b1(Q) 9. Na3+, draw.

5. Nc7 Kd6 6. Ne8+

Diagram 107

This is the only move: 6. Nb5+ Kc5 7. Nc7 b3 8. Ne6+ Kc4, and White loses.

> **6. ... Kc5 7. Nf6 Kd4 8. Ne8 b3 9. Nd6 Kc3 10. Ne4+ Kc2 11. Nd6 b2 12. Nc4 b1(Q) 13. Na3+, draw.**

Diagram 108
White to move

A good illustration of the defending capabilities of the knight—complete with checks and fork threats.

Note, however, that checks are not always helpful and not always available! Look at the position below.

Diagram 109
White to move

1. e6 Ne2+ 2. Kh2!

And the pawn strolls away from the pesky checks to its coronation. Note that 2. Kg4, taking the direct opposition on the diagonal, does not win due to 2. ... Nc3 3. e7 Nd5 4. e8(Q) Nf6+.

WHEN EACH SIDE HAS PAWNS, THE DECISIVE ROLE IS USUALLY PLAYED BY PASSED PAWNS. THREE ATTRIBUTES OF A PASSED PAWN ARE CRITICAL IN DETERMINING ITS POTENTIAL:

- how distant the passed pawn is;
- how movable it is;
- the effectiveness of its king support.

It is not always necessary to *defend* with the knight against the pawn. Let's look at a position that has been known for about nine centuries.

Diagram 110
White to move

Keep in mind that it's possible to mate a king with one knight only if the king is trapped in the corner by his own pawn.

1. Ng3+ Kh2 2. Nf5 Kh1 3. Kf2 Kh2 4. Ne3 Kh1 5. Nf1 h2 6. Ng3, mate.

Diagram 111

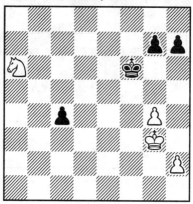

KORENSKY—SUETIN
RUSSIA, 1973

Diagram 112
Black to move

THE PLAN

When a defender has a distant passed pawn, exchanges on the other side of the board are usually helpful to him because they open lines for his king to penetrate. Furthermore, these exchanges may lead to the superior side retaining insufficient mating material.

THE PLAY

1. ... h5! 2. h3

The response 2. Nb4 allows 2. ... hxg4 3. Kxg4 Kg6, with a draw, because the knight must guard the c-pawn, and White's king cannot leave the kingside.

2. ... hxg4 3. hxg4 c3 4. Nb4 Kg5 5. Nc2 Kf6 6. Ne3 Kg6 7. Kf4 Kh6 8. Kf5 Kh7 9. Kg5 Kg8 10. Kg6 Kh8.

Diagram 113

11. Kg5

The approach White chooses doesn't promise much. But if 11. g5, then 11. ... Kg8 12. Nc2 Kh8 13. Kf7 Kh7 14. g6+ Kh8 =.

> **11. ... Kg8 12. Kf4 Kh7 13. Kf5 Kh6 14. Nc2 Kh7 15. Kg5 Kh8 16. Kg6 Kg8 17. Ne3 Kh8 18. Kf5 Kh7 19. Ke4 Kg6 20. Kd3 Kg5 21. Kxc3 Kf4, draw agreed.**

Diagram 114

An important position. White can't free his knight and defend his pawn at the same time.

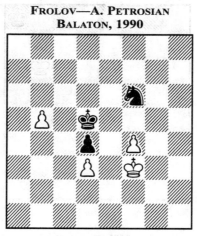

Diagram 115
White to move

White's passed b-pawn is his hoped-for salvation.

> **1. f5 Ke5 2. b6 Kxf5 3. b7 Nd7 4. Kg3 Nb8 5. Kf3 Nc6**
> **6. Kg3**

Now 6. ... Ke5 7. Kf3 Kd6 8. Ke4 Kc7 9. Kd5 Kxb7 10. Kc5.

Diagram 116
After 10. Kc5

This line leads to a drawish position similar to the
Korensky—Suetin game.

> **6. ... Nb8**

Diagram 117

7. Kf3 Nd7 8. Kg3 Ke5 9. Kf3 Kd6 10. Ke4 Kc5 11. Kf5 Kd6 12. Ke4 Kc5 13. Kf5, draw.

If 13. ... Kb4, then 14. Ke6, alternating attacks on both pawn and knight.

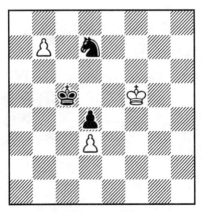

Diagram 118

MNATSAKANIAN—MOISEEV
MOSCOW, 1967

Diagram 119
White to move

Black is tied to the defense of his d6-pawn, and his passed pawns on the kingside become a target for White's pieces.

1. Ke3 g5

It is important not to let White's king get to f4, and then g5.

2. Kf3 Kf6

Zugzwang. If 2. ... Kd7, then 3. Ne3 f4 4. Nc4, followed by 5. Kg4, beginning to reap the pawn harvest.

3. Nxd6 g4+

3. ... Ke5 4. Nf7+ Kf6 5. Nh6 Ke5 6. d6 g4+ 7. Kf2 Ke6 8. Nxf5 +-.

4. hxg4 fxg4+ 5. Kf4 g3 6. Ne4+ Ke7 7. Ng5 Kd6
8. Ke4, Black resigns.

See Diagram 120, next page.

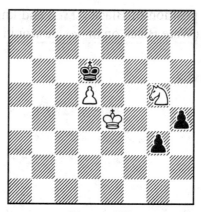

Diagram 120

Black is in zugzwang as soon as he runs out of king moves: 8. ... g2 9. Nh3 Kd7 10. Ke5 Ke7 11. d6+ Kd7 12. Kd5 Kd8 13. Ke6 Ke8 14. d7+ Kd8 15. Ng1!!.

In this example, the king was tied to the defense of his d6-pawn and could not support his passed pawns.

A "passer" is often created by means of a breakthrough.

ALBURT—LERNER
UKRAINE, 1978

Diagram 121
White to move

Because of the position of Black's king and knight, the break-through works. (Were Black on move, he would win easily with 1. ... Nd7.)

1. b4! axb4

If 1. ... cxb4, then 2. c5 b3+ 3. Kxb3 Ne4 4. Kc4+-. In case of 1. ... e4, then 2. bxc5 Kf2 3. c6 e3 4. d7 e2 5. d8(Q) e1(Q) 6. Qxf6+ is decisive. If 1. ... Nd7, White plays 2. bxa5 Kf2 3. a6 e4 4. a7 e3 5. a8(Q) e2 6. Qe4 e1(Q) 7. Qxe1+ Kxe1 8. a5 Nb8 9. Kc3, with the mortal threat of 10. a6. (But not the hasty 9. a6?, because of 9. ... Nxa6 10. d7

Diagram 122
After 10. d7

10. ... Nb4+ and 11. ... Nc6.)

2. a5 e4 3. a6 Kf2 4. a7 e3 5. a8(Q) e2

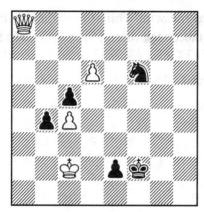

Diagram 123

After complications, the game morphs into a winning queen
ending for White.

> **6. Qf8 e1(Q) 7. Qxf6+ Kg3 8. Qg5+ Kh3 9. Qd2! Qa1**
> **10. d7 Qa4+ 11. Kb1 Qb3+ 12. Kc1 Qa3+**

12. ... Qxc4+ 13. Kb2+-.

> **13. Kd1 Qb3+ 14. Ke2 Kg4**

14. ... Qxc4+ 15. Qd3+.

Diagram 124

> **15. Qd1!**

This move forces the win, while the impatient 15. d8(Q) leads only to a perpetual check after 15. ... Qf3+ 16. Ke1 Qh1+ 17. Kf2 Qh2+ 18. Ke3 Qe5+ 19. Kd3 Qf5+.

15. ... Qxc4+ 16. Ke3+, Black resigns.

BISHOP VERSUS PAWNS

The bishop is usually more successful against the pawn (or pawns) than the knight is. It is seldom possible to limit the bishop's reach. The following example is a rare exception.

OTTEN

Diagram 125
White to move

White is winning thanks to exceptionally bad positioning of the Black king, which blocks its own bishop.

1. a5 Bf8 2. Kd5 Bh6 3. g5+! Bxg5

After 3. ... Kxg5 4. a6, the pawn is unstoppable.

4. Ke4

Diagram 126

4. ... Bh4 5. Kf3

The bishop can't get on the g1-a7 diagonal. Black is lost.

GAVRIKOV—CHIKOVANI
USSR, 1979

Diagram 127
White to move

1. Ka5

If 1. Kc5, then 1. ... Kf6 2. b4 (or 2. Kd6 Bd1 3. a5 Be2 =.
The bishop alone holds both pawns.) 2. ... Ke7 3. b5 Kd7 4.
Kb6 Bd1!—otherwise, 5. Ka7, winning—now if 5. a5, then

5. ... Be2, targeting the pawns, and Black holds.

Diagram 128
After 4. ... Bd1!

1. ... Kf6 2. b4 Ke5!

If 2. ... Ke7?, then 3. b5 Kd8 4. Ka6 Bd1 5. b6, with a win.

3. b5 Kd4!

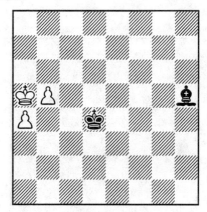

Diagram 129

Only attacking from behind achieves a draw here.

4. Kb6 Bf3 5. a5 Kc4 6. a6 Kb4 7. a7 Ba8, draw.

**WITH THE HELP OF ITS KING,
THE BISHOP CAN USUALLY REACH
A DRAW AGAINST TWO CONNECTED
PASSED PAWNS.**

Diagram 130

It can be difficult for a bishop alone to stop two isolated passed pawns.

SALVIOLI

Diagram 131
White to move

Here the bishop has to work on two fronts, guarding both of Black's pawns—and on different diagonals.

1. Bc4

If 1. Kg4, then 1. ... a3 2. Bc4 Kf2.

1. ... a3 2. Kg4 Kf2!

But not 2. ... d3, because of 3. Kf3.

3. Kf4 d3 4. Ke4 d2 5. Bb3 a2 6. Bxa2 d1(Q), winning.

❖ ❖ ♔ ❖ ❖

Diagram 132
White or Black to move

With White on move, Black is losing: 1. c5 Be5 2. c6 Kd2 3. f6 Ke3 4. f7 Bd6 5. c7. But if it's Black to move, it's an easy draw, because the bishop has time to create a defensive line guarding both pawns on one diagonal (a3-f8):

1. ... Bd6! 2. Kb2 Kd2 3. Kb3 Kd3 4. f6 Bc5 5. f7 Bf8 with a draw.

❖ ❖ ♔ ❖ ❖

WHENEVER POSSIBLE, PASSED PAWNS SHOULD BE STOPPED ON THE SAME DIAGONAL.

The match between bishop and three pawns often ends in favor of the pawns, although even here there are many examples of successful defense.

HORWITZ

Diagram 133
Black to move

Another useful defensive technique: the bishop attacks pawns from the rear.

White reaches a drawn position whichever pawn check Black tries. King moves don't win either: on 1. ... Kf5, White waits with 2. Bd8; and on 1. ... Kh5, 2. Bd6 stops the pawn advance.

1. ... f3+

Or, 1. ... h3+ 2. Kh2 f3 3. Bc5 Kf4 (3. ... Kh4 4. Bf2+ Kg4 5. Bg3=) 4. Kxh3 g4+ 5. Kh4 g3 6. Bd6+ Ke3 7. Bxg3, draw.

2. Kf2 Kf4 3. Bxg5+

Also possible is 3. Bd8, leading to ... h3 4. Bc7+ Ke4 5. Bb8 =.

3. ... Kxg5 4. Kxf3, draw.

Let's look at some bishop-versus-pawn endgames from tournament practice to see how these principles are put to use.

MARIC—SILADY
NOVI SAD, 1973

Diagram 134
White to Move

Thanks to the active position of his king, White can successfully neutralize and capture the ominous-looking mass of Black pawns.

1. Bc6 b3

If 1. ... a3, then 2. Ba4 Kf6 3. Bc2 g5 4. fxg5+ Kxg5 5. Kd4, and White has enough time to take all Black's queenside pawns, and to neutralize his opponent's f-pawn with his bishop.

2. a3! b2 3. Be4 f5 4. Bc2 Kh6 5. Kd4

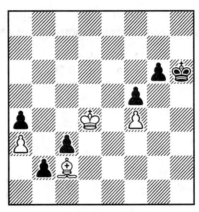

Diagram 135

5. ... Kh5

5. ... g5 6. fxg5+ Kxg5 7. Kxc3 f4 8. Kxb2 f3 9. Kc3 f2 10. Bd3 +-.

6. Kxc3 Kg4 7. Kxb2 Kxf4 8. Bxa4 g5 9. Bc6 g4 10. a4 Ke5.

Diagram 136

11. Kc3!

It is important to limit the actions of Black's king.

11. ... Kd6 12. Bb7 Kc7 13. Bg2, winning.

White has an easy win—for example, 13. ... f4 14. Be4 Kb6 15. Kb4 Ka7 16. Kb5 f3 17. a5 f2 18. Bg2 g3 19. a6 Kb8 20. Kb6.

**CAPABLANCA—EM. LASKER
NEW YORK, 1924**

**Diagram 137
White to move**

White has a big advantage, thanks to the kingside pawns supported by his king.

1. Kg4!

The most precise. If 1. Ke5?, then 1. ... Kg6.

1. ... Bc4 2. f5 Bb3 3. Kf4 Bc2 4. Ke5 Kf7 5. a4!

Played to create a third passed pawn.

5. ... Kg7 6. d5

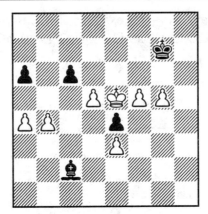

Diagram 138

6. ... Bxa4

Or 6. ... cxd5 7. Kxd5 Bxa4 8. Kxe4.

7. d6 c5 8. bxc5 Bc6 9. Ke6 a5 10. f6+, Black resigns.

ROOK AGAINST PAWN

In endings with rook against pawn, the pawn's distance from its promotion square and position of both kings are key factors.

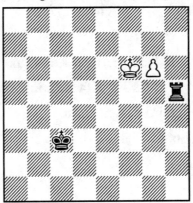

Diagram 139
White to move

1. g7 Rh6+ 2. Kf5

2. Kf7 Rh7 = ; or 2. Kg5 Rh1 =.

2. ... Rh5+ 3. Kf4 Rh4+ 4. Kf3 Rh3+ 5. Kg2, and White wins.

CUTTING OFF THE KING ON HIS THIRD RANK

Diagram 140
White to move

Black's king and pawn are almost at the starting position. This fact allows White to use an important technique—putting his rook on Black's fourth rank to keep the enemy king limited to his own third rank.

1. Rg5

Black's king is cut off.

Now pushing the pawn makes no sense because, if it reached Black's 6th rank, it would be attacked by the rook from g3 and would be lost after ... c2 and Rc3. (See Diagram 141.) That's why the Black king should choose the long way around, but this route takes time.

1. ... c5 2. Kd8 Kc6 3. Ke7 Kb5 4. Kd6, winning.

While we're on this subject, here's another very important position.

Diagram 141

Here the obvious difference with Diagram 140 is that Black's pawn has already advanced to his fifth rank. With the move, Black draws by playing 1. ... Kd5, crossing his vital fourth rank. White to move plays, without the need for any calculation, 1. Rg5—cutting off the king and winning.

If you can't cut off the opponent's king on its fourth rank, the outcome of the game depends on the effectiveness of the cooperation among the pieces of each army. There are even rules of opposition in these endings—similar to those in pawn endings. The techniques of "passing the move" and "the running screen," which we saw in king and pawn endings, are important here as well.

Diagram 142
White to move

White can win if he can bring his king to attack the pawn, but his opponent's king is in the way, using vertical opposition. After the natural 1. Rd1 d4 2. Kd7 Kd5, White does not gain anything—for example, 3. Rd2 Kc4 4. Ke6 Kc3 (winning a decisive tempo) 5. Rd1 d3 6. Ke5 Kc2 7. Rh1 d2, with a draw.

1. Rd2!

A hard-to-find, tempo-losing but game-winning move that forces Black to relinquish the opposition, allowing White's king into the action.

1. ... d4 2. Rd1! Ke4

Or 2. ... Kd5 3. Kd7!, then moving to the opposite side of that chosen by Black's king, for example—3. ... Ke4 4. Kc6, etc.

3. Kd6 d3 4. Kc5 Ke3 5. Kc4 d2 6. Kc3, winning.

Here's another example where the opposition rules.

PANCHENKO

Diagram 143
White or Black to move

With White to move, the game's a draw: 1. Kc7 Kc5 or 1. Rb2 (too close for comfort!) 1. ... Kc4 2. Kb6 Kc3 3. Rh2 b3 4. Kb5 b2. But if it's Black's move, he has to give up the opposition and let White's king in.

1. ... Kc4

Or 1. ... Ka4 2. Kb6 +-.

2. Kb6 b3 3. Ka5 Kc3 4. Ka4 b2 5. Ka3, winning.

THE RUNNING SCREEN
IN ROOK–VERSUS–PAWN ENDINGS

Here the running screen—when one king "shoulders" out another king from key squares—familiar to us from Chapter 2, prevents the enemy king from getting to a pawn. This technique is doubly advantageous because you can advance to the important squares while blocking your opponent from doing so.

PANCHENKO

Diagram 144
Black to move

1. ... Ke4

The only move that leads to a draw. 1. ... Kf4 loses to 2. Kd4
Kf3 3. Kd3 g3 4. Rf7+ Kg2 5. Ke2 Kh2 6. Rg7 g2 7. Kf2.

2. Rg7 Kf3 3. Kd4 g3 4. Kd3 g2, draw.

**IF THE PAWN IS ON THE SEVENTH RANK
AND CAN'T BE STOPPED BY JOINT
EFFORT OF ROOK AND KING,
OR—IDEALLY—BLOCKED
BY THE KING, THE GAME
IS USUALLY A DRAW.**

Let's look at one important exception to the rule at the bottom of page 119.

Diagram 145
White to move

1. Kb3 a1(N)+

Under-promotion of the pawn to a knight is forced because of the threat of mate.

2. Kc3

Black is in zugzwang. White wins. But move all the pieces in Diagram 145 one square to the right, and underpromotion draws.

TWO CONNECTED PAWNS
VERSUS THE ROOK

Two connected and far-advanced pawns often successfully challenge an unsupported rook. But first note that if the side with the rook gets his king in front of the pawns, he usually wins.

IN CASES LIKE DIAGRAM **145,**
PROMOTING THE PAWN TO A
KNIGHT ON ALL NON-ROOK FILES
SAVES THE DAY!

Diagram 146   **Diagram 147**

**Black wins easily in both cases—even when the pawns
are advanced all the way to the sixth rank.**

In the next example, the position of the White king makes all
the difference.

**TARRASCH—JANOWSKI
OSTENDE, 1907**

Diagram 148
White to move

1. Kd4 Kb3

1. ... Rf5 2. Ke4 Rxg5 3. f7 Rg4+ 4. Ke3+-.

2. Ke5 Kc4 3. g6 Re1+ 4. Kd6 Rd1+ 5. Ke7 Re1+ 6. Kf7, winning.

The king must be placed correctly to fight such dangerously advanced pawns to a draw.

Diagram 149
Black to move

Although the Black king is on his way to the pawns, a straight-forward approach is a mistake—for example, if 1. ... Kd4 2. Kg7 Ke5 3. f6 Ke6 4. f7 +-. From the start, it is important to prevent White's king from getting to g7, and then pushing the f-pawn to f7, as the closer f-pawn and not the farther-away g-pawn is the easier target for Black's king.

1. ... Rf3! 2. Ke5

Or 2. g7 Rg3 3. Kf7 Kd4 4. f6 Ke5 5. Ke7 Rg6, with a draw.

2. ... Rg3! 3. f6

THE ROOK ALONE CAN'T STOP TWO CONNECTED PAWNS IF BOTH REACH THE SIXTH RANK.

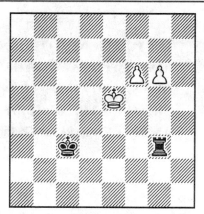

Diagram 150
Black to move

3. ... Rg5+

The only saving move—and on some occasions missed even by
GMs. After 4. Ke6 Rxg6 or 4. Ke4 Rxg6, it's a draw.

ARULAID—GURGENIDZE
UKRAINE, 1956

Diagram 151

Against such menacing pawns, White's only defense is attack!

1. Kd6 Kc8 2. Rc1+ Kb7 3. Rb1+ Ka6 4. Kc6 Ka5
5. Kc5 Ka4 6. Kc4 Ka3 7. Kc3 Ka2 8. Rf1

White's king is "shadowing" Black's king. Now 8. ... g2 is
impossible—9. Rxf2+; White can reach the pawns on time.

IN POSITIONS WITH ROOK AGAINST
CONNECTED PAWNS, THE TECHNIQUE
OF "SHADOWING" THE OPPONENT'S
KING ON THE EDGE OF THE BOARD
CAN BE A LIFE-SAVING, LAST RESORT.

Diagram 152

8. ... h5 9. Kd3 h4 10. Ke3 h3 11. Kf3

Or 11. Rxf2+.

11. ... g2 12. Rxf2+, draw.

In positions with rook against three pawns, the rook usually
wins if the king is in the way of the pawns and if those pawns
are not too far advanced. Otherwise, the pawns can draw or
even win. The following position, analyzed more than 150
years ago, is important to know.

Diagram 153
White to move

1. Rf2 Kg6

Clearly, it's White who enjoys winning chances. Black must play well to hold.

2. Kf4 Kf6 3. Re2 Kf7

It is possible here to abandon the f5-pawn: 4. Kxf5? g3!.

4. Re5 Kg6 5. Re6+

But not 5. Rxf5 h2 6. Rg5+ Kh6.

Diagram 154
Black to move

5. ... Kg7

Here 5. ... Kh5? loses because of 6. Rd6 (zugzwang) 6. ... h2 7. Rd8, and 5. ... Kh7? loses to 6. Kg5 g3 7. Rh6+.

6. Rd6 Kf7 7. Rh6 Kg7 8. Rh5

If 8. Kg5, then 8. ... f4!.

8. ... Kg6 9. Rg5+ Kh6 10. Rg8

The f5 pawn is untouchable because of ... h2.

10. ... Kh7 11. Rd8 Kg6 12. Rd6+ Kf7

Draw by repetition. But notice that if we move all of the pieces in Diagram 154 one row "up," White wins easily. If we move them one row "down," White loses (see Exercise 6, Diagram 169).

QUEEN VERSUS PAWNS

The queen is so powerful that it normally handles even multiple pawns with ease. But there are positions when even a single pawn can draw.

Diagram 155
White to move

Using checks, White forces his opponent's king to take a square ahead of the pawn. This technique gains White time to approach with his own king.

>**1. Qf4+ Kg2 2. Qe3 Kf1 3. Qf3+ Ke1 4. Kc5 Kd2 5. Qf4+ Kd1 6. Qd4+ Kc2 7. Qe3**

THE QUEEN USUALLY TAKES CARE OF THE PAWNS EASILY, ESPECIALLY WHEN IT OPPOSES A SINGLE PAWN— EXCEPT IN THE CASE OF A ROOK- OR BISHOP-PAWN ALREADY ON THE SEVENTH RANK.

Diagram 156

7. ... Kd1 8. Qd3+ Ke1 9. Kd4 Kf2 10. Qe3+ Kf1 11. Qf3+ Ke1 12. Kd3, winning.

This is a winning technique that always works against pawns located on the b-, d-, e- and g-files.

THIS METHOD OF WINNING A TEMPO BY DRIVING THE WEAKER KING IN FRONT OF HIS OWN PAWN DOESN'T WORK WITH ROOK- AND BISHOP-PAWNS (A-, C-, F-, AND H-PAWNS) BECAUSE OF STALEMATE OPPORTUNITIES.

Diagram 157
White to move

1. Qb4+ Kc2 2. Qa3 Kb1 3. Qb3+

Diagram 158

3. ... Ka1, draw.

If White's king takes the opportunity to approach, it's a stalemate. So White can't improve his position.

But an extra pawn can doom this defense. Let's add a pawn to Diagram 157:

Diagram 159
White to move

1.Qb4+ Kc2 2. Qa3 Kb1 3. Qb3+ Ka1

Diagram 160

4. Qc2! h4 5. Qc1 mate.

Diagram 161
White to move

Another position where the stalemate defense makes it impossible for White to win time to bring his king closer.

1. Qd2 Kb1 2. Qb4+ Ka2 3. Qc3 Kb1 4. Qb3+

Diagram 162

4. ... Ka1 5. Qxc2 stalemate.

When the king is close enough to attack with mate threats, the superior side can win.

Diagram 163
White to move

1. Qd4+ Kc1 2. Qb4!

White prevents the Black king from getting to the a1 square, stalemate haven.

2. ... Kd1 3. Qb3 Kd2 4. Qb2 Kd1 5. Kf3! Kd2

If 5. ... c1(Q), 6. Qe2 mate.

6. Ke4 Kd1 7. Kd3 c1(Q) 8. Qe2 mate.

Summary: Endgames are most often decided because a pawn reaches its promotion square. The slow-moving knight has a tougher time against a pawn than do other pieces. Passed a- and h-pawns are particularly difficult for the knight. (However, a lone knight on the seventh rank in front of an enemy rook-pawn on the sixth can hold off both the pawn and the enemy king. Bishop-and center-pawns are easiest for the knight because it's off the "rim" and not so "dim." When both sides have pawns, passed pawns are critical. Three factors determine their potential—how distant and how movable they are, and the position of the pieces, especially the kings.

The bishop is usually more successful against a pawn or pawns than the knight. Whenever possible, pawns should be stopped on one diagonal. With some help from its king, a bishop can usually reach a draw against two connected passed pawns. But it is more difficult for the bishop alone to stop two isolated pawns, working on two fronts on different diagonals. Three pawns often beat the bishop, but sometimes there are still successful defensive techniques.

In rook against pawn, the pawn's distance from its promotion square and the position of the two kings are crucial factors. Cutting off the king by putting the rook on its fifth rank is an effective winning technique. If a pawn is on the seventh and can't be blocked by the enemy king, or stopped by the joint effort of king and rook, the game is usually drawn. Two connected, far-advanced pawns often challenge a rook, but if the side with the rook gets his king in front of the pawns, he generally wins. Likewise, against three passed pawns, the rook most often wins if its king helps stop the pawns, as long as the pawns are not too far advanced.

A queen normally handles pawns easily. But even a single rook- or bishop-pawn on the seventh rank can sometimes draw because of stalemating possibilities.

Pawns against Pieces
Learning Exercises

Diagram 164
Black to move

Diagram 165
White to move

Diagram 166
White to move

Diagram 167
White to move

Diagram 168
Black to move

Diagram 169
Black to move

Diagram 170
White to move

Diagram 171
Black to move

Pawns against Pieces
Solutions

No. 1   **1. ... Kb5!** (1. ... Bc5 2. Nb8 a5 3. Nc6 and 4. Nxa5 =)
2. Nxa7+ Kc5 3. Nc8 a5 4. Ne7 a4 5. Nf5 a3
6. Ne3 a2 7. Nc2 Kc4 -+.

No. 2   **1. c4! Nxc4+ 2. Kc3 Nd6** (2. ... Nb6 3. Kd4) **3. b6 Kf6 4. b7 +-.**

No. 3   **1. e4 Bxe4 2. Kf7 Ke2 3. Ke6 Ke3 4. Ke5**
(opposition and zugzwang) **4. ... Kd3 5. d5 +-** or
4. ... Kf3 5. f5 +-.

No. 4   **1. Bf5 Kg7 2. Be6 Kxg6 3. Bb3! axb3+**
(3. ... a3 4. Bc4 Kf5 5. Kb3 Ke5 6. Kxb4 +-)
4. Kxb3 Kf6 5. Kxb4 Ke6 6. Kxc3 Kd5 7. Kb4 +-.

No. 5   **1. ... Kd5! 2. Kc7 Kc5 3. Kb7 Kb5 4. Rb1+ Kc5 5. Ka6 c3 =.**

No. 6   **1. ... f3+ 2. Rxf3** (2. Kh1 g2+ 3. Kxh2 gxf1(N)+
[or 3. ... gxf1(B)]) **2. ... h1(Q)+ 3. Kxh1 Kxf3 4. Kg1 g2 -+.**

No. 7   **1. Kb6 Kb2 2. Kc5+ Kc2 3. Qg2+ Kb1 4. Kb4 a1(Q)**
5. Kb3 Qf6 6. Qc2+ (or 6. Qg1+) **+-.**

No. 8   **1. ... Ka1** (1. ... Kb1? 2. Kb4 c1(Q) 3. Kb3 +-)
2. Qd2 Kb1 3. Qd3 (3. Kb4 c1[Q])
3. ... Kb2 4. Qe2 Ka1! =.

Chapter 4: Rook Endings
Some Important Ideas to Look For

◆ Philidor's position

Black plays 1. ... Rb6 to draw easily.
See Diagram 175.

◆ Building a Lucena bridge to win

White has just played 5. Re4!.
See Diagram 179.

◆ The long-side defense

Black plays 3. ... Ra1!.
See Diagram 183.

◆ Greater piece activity can overcome material disadvantage.

Black plays 1. ... Rd2!
See Diagram 222.

Chapter 4
Rook Endings:
Long-Range Artillery

G rab the remote and push "mute." This chapter will be important to half of the endgames you play, because rook endings make up 50% of all endgames played in tournament chess! In Chapter 3 you've just learned the important techniques in endgames involving rook vs. one or more pawns. Now you need to know the ideas and a few key positions that are crucial when

rook battles rook with pawns on the board. Staying sharp in both pawn endings (Chapter 2) and rook endings is one of the most time-efficient investments you can make to better your results in tournament chess. So, when you finish the first four chapters of this book, you will have already made a significant advance in your knowledge—and your increased understanding is sure to lead to more victories!

ROOK AND PAWN VS. ROOK, WITH THE DEFENDING KING BLOCKING THE PAWN

Let's look first at rook and single pawn against the lone rook. As in king and pawn endings, the defending king's first choice should be to get in front of the enemy pawn to block its path.

PAWN IS ON THE SIXTH RANK

In positions where the stronger side's pawn has reached the sixth (or Black's third) rank, and the opponent's king is blocking its way, the following ideas and techniques are important.

ZEPLER

Diagram 172
White to move

Even here, when White has many advantages—including a passive Black rook, and a tremendous spatial advantage, the game is drawn because White can't strengthen his position.

ROOK ENDGAMES, WITHOUT OTHER PIECES, ARE THE SECOND-MOST DRAWISH ENDINGS. BISHOPS OF OPPOSITE COLOR ARE THE MOST DRAWISH. AS USUAL, THE MORE PAWNS ON THE BOARD, THE GREATER THE CHANCES OF WINNING.

**"PASSIVE DEFENSE"—BUILDING
A FORTRESS AND STAYING WITHIN
IT—WORKS AGAINST A KNIGHT
OR ROOK PAWN.**

1. Rh7+ Kg8 2. Rg7+ Kh8!

The alternative, 2. ... Kf8, loses after 3. Kh7 and 4. Rf7+. (See the Lucena position, Diagram 178.)

The results are different if you move the entire position over one square from the corner.

Diagram 173
White to move

1. Rc7 Rb8 2. Rg7+ Kf8

Or 2. ... Kh8 3. Rh7+ Kg8 4. f7+ Kf8 5. Rh8+.

3. Rh7 Kg8 4. f7+, winning.

**THE RESULTS ARE DIFFERENT WITH
CENTER AND BISHOP PAWNS—
"PASSIVE DEFENSE" DOESN'T WORK!**

White could conduct the winning maneuver because Black's rook had to remain passive on the back rank to protect his king from checkmate. Passive defense—where the defender's rook is lifeless on the back rank—doesn't work here.

If we change the position slightly, putting White's king on e6, the position is a draw because Black can activate his rook.

Diagram 174
White to move

Pawn is not yet on the sixth rank — Philidor's position

If the pawn has not reached the sixth rank, the weaker side should aim for what chess masters call "Philidor's Position," guaranteeing an easy draw. More than 200 years ago, Andre Philidor realized the importance of the following position.

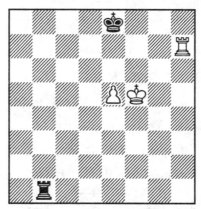

Diagram 175
Black to move

Diagram 175 represents one of those "generic" or matrix positions that can be moved to the left or right, up or down the board. The method even works with rook-pawns, although then the defender has a simpler, passive defense we've already seen as an alternative.

White has achieved a lot. His king and pawn are advanced to the fifth rank, and his rook limits Black's king to his back rank. White threatens to bring his king (remember, generally you want to advance your king first) to the sixth rank, where it would add mating threats to Black's problems, eventually chasing the defending king from his guard of the queening square.

But despite all of these advantages, the position is a basic, building-block draw! (Rook endings are drawish!) Remember this key position and practice with it! Philidor worked out a method that splits the point easily, illustrating the drawing power of the rook. This three-part technique is now part of every chess master's knowledge:

1. ... Rb6

Step 1. Black keeps White's king off the sixth rank.

2. e6

Or 2. Rg7 Ra6 3. Rg6 Rxg6 4. Kxg6 Ke7=.

2. ... Rb1!

Step 2. After White pushes his pawn to the sixth rank, Black's rook immediately drops all the way "back" to harass the White king from the rear.

3. Kf6 Rf1+ 4. Ke5 Re1+

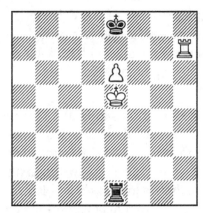

Diagram 176

5. Kd6 Rd1+, draw.

PHILIDOR'S METHOD

1. THE DEFENDER PREVENTS HIS OPPONENT'S KING FROM ADVANCING TO THE SIXTH RANK. SO THE SUPERIOR SIDE IS FORCED TO PUSH HIS PAWN TO USE IT AS SHELTER TO CROSS THE SIXTH.

2. AT THAT POINT THE DEFENDER SHIFTS HIS ROOK TO THE REAR—USUALLY ALL THE WAY TO THE FIRST RANK—IN ORDER TO GIVE CHECKS.

3. WITH THE PAWN ON THE SIXTH, THE ATTACKER'S KING CAN'T ESCAPE THE CHECKS FROM BEHIND, SO HE ISN'T ABLE TO CREATE THE MATING THREATS NEEDED TO CHASE THE DEFENDING KING OFF THE QUEENING SQUARE.

LUCENA'S POSITION

Now let's look at rook vs. rook-and-pawn positions where the Black king is pushed out of the pawn's way. Here the White king has already managed to reach the seventh rank.

Diagram 177
White to move

Nothing can stop White from winning. But he has to know the only proper technique. This is another position that you should know very well—a position which can lead by force to "Lucena's position," also hundreds of years old and named after the author of the oldest existing chess book, published in 1497. Interestingly, the manuscript doesn't include this position! White can win by a technique Aaron Nimzovitch later dubbed "building a bridge." White configures a straight line of rook, king and pawn on the file, escaping checks and ensuring that the pawn can "cross" to its queening square.

First, White advances his pawn as far as possible.

1. Kh7 Rh2+ 2. Kg8 Rg2 3. g7

LUCENA'S POSITION

Diagram 178

3. ... Rh2

Or 3. ... Rg3 4. Rh1 Kf6 5. Kh8 Rxg7 6. Rf1+ Kg6 7. Rg1+ with the win.

WINNING BY "BUILDING A BRIDGE"

1. **THE SUPERIOR SIDE ADVANCES HIS PAWN TO THE SEVENTH RANK TO REACH LUCENA'S POSITION.**

2. **HE USES HIS ROOK TO PUSH HIS OPPONENT'S KING OUT OF THE WAY.**

3. **HE ADVANCES HIS ROOK TO THE FOURTH RANK.**

4. **HE MOVES HIS OWN KING OUT OF THE WAY OF HIS PAWN.**

5. **HE ADVANCES HIS KING TOWARD THE OPPONENT'S CHECKING ROOK UNTIL REACHING THE FIFTH RANK.**

6. **HE INTERPOSES HIS ROOK TO BLOCK THE CHECK, COMPLETING THE "BRIDGE."**

4. Re1+ Kd7

To make progress, White needs to move his king out of the way of his pawn. Moving the king immediately accomplishes nothing: 5. Kf7 Rf2+ 6. Kg6 Rg2+ 7. Kf6 Rf2+ 8. Ke5 Rg2, and the king has to come back. However …

5. Re4!

Played to be able to provide a future shelter for the king.

Diagram 179

5. ... Rh1 6. Kf7 Rf1+ 7. Kg6 Rg1+ 8. Kh6

The threat is 9. Re5 and 10. Rg5, building a bridge, or 9. Rh4 and 10. Kh7. That's why Black couldn't wait to check again.

8. ... Rh1+ 9. Kg5 Rg1+ 10. Rg4

The "bridge," which is really a block against checks, has been completed and White wins easily. (See diagram, next page.)

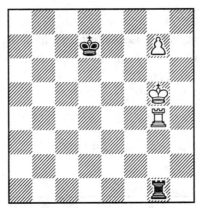

Diagram 180

COUNTERATTACKING FROM THE SIDE—THE LONG-SIDE DEFENSE

Even when Philidor's defense is no longer available, the weaker side shouldn't give up. Other drawing techniques are often successful.

Diagram 181
Black to move

As we've seen in Chapter 2, without the rooks on the board this is a basic and simple win. But the rooks, as usual, add drawing potential!

White threatens mate. Black's king has to leave the queening square, but which way should it go? The move 1. ... Ke8 loses after 2. Ra8+ Kd7. (See Diagram 182 on page 148.)

Strongest player of the 18th Century

In Analysis of the Game of Chess, *he was first to write about the key principles of winning chess middlegame play and to analyze a basic endgame.*

◆ Leading operatic composer of his day

◆ Amazed European audiences with blindfold displays

◆ Remembered with "Philidor's Legacy," "Philidor's Defense," and "Philidor's Position"

Master of the Endgame
Andre Philidor

Place of Birth: Paris
Date of Birth: September 7, 1726

Andre Philidor was a man equally brilliant in two fields, music and chess. In fact, some of his contemporaries, aware of his chess exploits, incorrectly doubted that he was the true composer of some of his operas!

Philidor was certainly the 18th Century's best player. For half that century he was the unofficial world champion, successfully giving odds to the next-strongest players in the world. Nevertheless, he remained a chess amateur, turning to chess full time only after 20 years as France's leading operatic composer. Along the way, he wrote his famous *Analysis of Chess.*

In his last years, he was a victim of the paranoia resulting from the French Revolution. Because his name was placed on the "enemies list," he could not safely return to France. Philidor died August 31, 1795 in England, where he is buried in Piccadilly. The letter he had been anxiously awaiting for years, clearance to come home to his family, arrived too late.

Philidor was at least 200 years ahead of his time in his understanding of chess. At a time when flashy, foolhardy play dominated, he coined the term "Pawns are the soul of chess."

Diagram 182
After 2. ... Kd7

3. Rf8 (not 3. Kg6 Ke7!, preventing f6, and White has nothing better than going back to the original position: 4. Ra7+ Kf8 5. Kf6) 3. ... Rf2 (or 3. ... Rh1 4. Kg7! and Black's rook doesn't have enough room for the last resort, a successful attack from the side.) 4. Kg7!—White is going to reach the Lucena position.

From Diagram 181, Black can draw by employing an important defensive technique—the long-side defense.

1. ... Kg8! 2. Ra8+ Kh7 3. Rf8

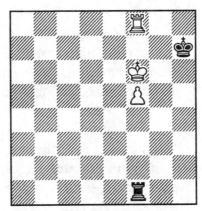

Diagram 183

The only way White can start to advance his pawn—but now Black's rook heads decisively for the "long side."

3. ... Ra1! 4. Re8

If 4. Ke6, 4. ... Kg7!.

4. ... Rf1

Once White's rook leaves the f-file, the Black rook occupies it, preventing the pawn advance.

5. Re7+ Kg8 6. Ra7 Rf2 7. Ra8+ Kh7 8. Ke6 Kg7!, drawing.

Diagram 184

THE LONG-SIDE DEFENSE

BLACK DRAWS BY RETREATING HIS KING TO THE SHORTER SIDE (FROM THE PAWN'S PERSPECTIVE) OF THE BOARD, AND MOVING HIS ROOK TO THE LONGER SIDE TO COUNTERATTACK WITH CHECKS.

A successful long-side defense depends on controlling the eighth rank at the right time.

Diagram 185
Black to move

1. ... Ra7+ 2. Rd7

If 2. Ke8, 2. ... Kf6, draw.

2. ... Ra8!

All other moves, for example 2. ... Ra6, lose (3. Ke8+ and 4. e7).

3. Rc7 Kg6

Or 3. Rd8 Ra7+ 4. Ke8 Kf6, draw.

Black holds, although not without some difficulty.

WHEN THE LONG SIDE IS TOO SHORT

GRIGORIEV

Diagram 186
Black to move

Here the Black rook doesn't have enough room to successfully use a long-side defense. The distance between it and the pawn is only two squares. Even on move, Black loses.

1. ... Rb8+

On 1. ... Ra2, 2. Rg1+ Kf6 (or 2. ... Kh7 Rg4, building the bridge and winning) 3. Kf8 wins.

2. Kd7 Rb7+ 3. Kd6 Rb8

Or 3. ... Rb6+ 4. Kc7 Re6 5. Kd7.

4. Kc7 Ra8

Diagram 187

5. Ra1!

If White did not have this last move, or if Black were on move, the game would be a draw because there are now three squares between the rook and pawn—the normal maneuvering room required for a successful "long-side" defense.

5. ... Re8 6. Kd7, winning.

THE DEFENDING KING IS CUT OFF FROM THE PAWN

If the weaker side's king is cut off from the pawn, the frontal attack is the most effective—and often the only—method of defense.

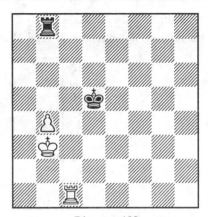

Diagram 188
White to move

With the rook in front, it is also important to have a three-square interval between the rook and pawn. A smaller interval usually leads to a loss.

1. Ka4 Ra8+ 2. Kb5 Rb8+ 3. Ka5 Ra8+!

There should not be any pause between the checks.

4. Kb6 Rb8+ 5. Ka5 Ra8+ 6. Kb5 Rb8+ 7. Ka4 Ra8+

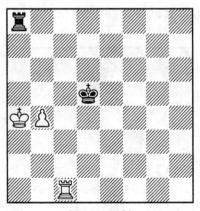

Diagram 189

To escape the checks, White's king has to drop back to b3.

From Diagram 188, rook moves do not help White either. For

example: 1. Rc5+ Kd6 2. Ka4 (2. Kc4 Rh8) 2. ... Ra8+ 3. Kb5 (3. Ra5 Rb8 4. b5 Kc5 =) 3. ... Rb8+ 4. Kc4 Rh8.

Diagram 190
After 4. ... Rh8

Back to Diagram 188, after 1. Rc4, the threat is that White's king can move forward without worrying about his pawn. But after 1. ... Kd6 2. Ka4 Kd5 3. Rc5+ (or 3. Rc7 Kd6 4. Ra7 Kc6=) 3. ... Kd6 4. Ka5 Ra8+ 5. Kb5 Rb8+, we reach the same drawn position we saw earlier.

If the stronger side is able to protect his pawn with the rook, he usually wins.

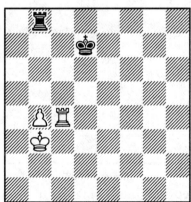

Diagram 191
White to move

1. Ka4 Ra8+

If 1. ... Rc8 2. Rxc8 Kxc8 3. Ka5 +-.

**2. Kb5 Rb8+ 3. Ka6 Ra8+ 4. Kb7 Ra4 5. Rc7+,
White wins.**

WHEN THE EXTRA PAWN IS A ROOK-PAWN
As is in pawn endgames, the rook-pawn is the most drawish in
rook endgames, so the defense is easiest with this pawn. The
following are key positions.

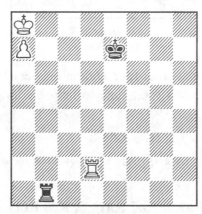

Diagram 192
White to move

This is a draw, because White's rook can't help his king get out
of the corner to make way for the pawn.

**1. Rh2 Kd7 2. Rh8 Kc7 3. Rb8 Rc1 4. Rb7+ Kc8,
draw.**

Chess is a game of understanding,
not of memory.
—Znosko-Borovsky

Diagram 193
White to move

The horizontal interval of four squares between the king and the pawn allows White's rook time to help his king out from the corner.

1. Rc2 Ke7 2. Rc8 Kd6

Or 2. ... Kd7 3. Rb8 Ra1 4. Kb7 Rb1+ 5. Ka6 Ra1+ 6. Kb6 Rb1+ 7. Kc5+-.

3. Rb8 Ra1 4. Kb7 Rb1+ 5. Kc8 Rc1+ 6. Kd8 Rh1

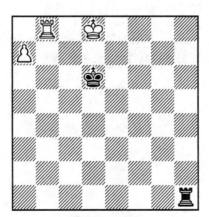

Diagram 194
7. Rb6+! Kc5 8. Rc6+!

White wins—for example, if 8. ... Kxc6 then 9. a8(Q)+; or 8. ...
Kd5 9. Ra6; finally, if 8. ... Kb5 9. Rc8.

Let's take a look at the following important position, where the
king can't aid in the defense—and the superior side's rook is in
front of his pawn, which has been advanced to the seventh.

Diagram 195
Black to move

Here, Black draws easily with 1. ... Rb1, putting his rook
behind the pawn. As White's king approaches the b7-pawn to
free up his rook, Black checks with his rook from the "bottom"
of the board, and then returns to the b-file. With White's king
away from his pawn, Black can also kill time by shuffling back
and forth on the h7-g7 squares. (But he can't approach any closer. If 1. ... Rb1 2. Kd6 Kf7? 3. Rh8 Rxb7 4. Rh7+.) This method
of defense also works with the pawns on the other files.

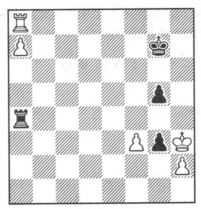

Diagram 196
White to move

In this position White played 1. hxg3?, and after 1. ... g4+ 2. fxg4, the two additional pawns (g3 and g4) do not win. White's pawn can reach g6, but Black's rook moves along the a-file or gives checks (if White's king threatens to support his pawn on a7), and thus does not allow the opponent's rook to leave the a8-square. But White has a better move.

1. Kxg3! Kh7 2. h4! gxh4+ 3. Kh3 Kg7 4. f4

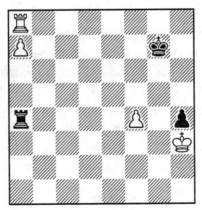

Diagram 197

4. ... Kh7

If 4. ... Rxf4?, then 5. Rb8.

5. f5 Kg7 6. f6+ Kxf6 7. Rf8+, winning.

Or 6. ... Kf7 7. Rh8 Rxa7 8. Rh7+, wins. With the a-, b-, or c-pawn on the seventh, the only safe kingside squares for Black's king are g7 and h7. Therefore, an extra h- or g-pawn would not win for White, since he can't deny Black both safe squares. On the other hand, an extra pawn on any other file would win.

Diagram 198	Diagram 199

The great Tarrasch, one of the original grandmasters, taught that positions like 198 are drawn and those like 199 are a win. Later players discovered *both* were drawn.

Diagram 198 has long been known to be a draw because Black's king can simply advance on the pawn—for example, 1. ... Kf7 2. b7 Kg7!, or 2. Kg2 Ke7! 3. b7 Kd7—just in time.

But until the early 20th Century, the position in Diagram 199 was thought to be won for White. His king marches to hide on a7, while Black's king cannot help because it cannot cross the mined e-file—for example, 1. ... Kf7 2. Kg2 Ke7? 3. a7 and White wins.

But Vanchura discovered a drawing technique that even today some GMs have failed to employ to save games! From Diagram 199, with White to move, the game may continue 1. Kg2 Ra5 2. Kf3 Rf5+ 3. Ke4 Rf6, leading to the following Vanchura position.

VANCHURA

Diagram 200
White to move

White's rook is tied to defending his pawn. His king would like to hide on a7, but is prevented by checks from the side.

1. Kd5 Rf5+ 2. Kc4 Rf6 3. Kb5

3. a7 Ra6 =.

3. ... Rf5+ 4. Kb6 Rf6+ 5. Ka7 Rf7+
6. Kb6 Rf6+, draw.

Courtesy www.chesscafe.com

Aron Nimzovitch (1886-1935), the self-described "crown prince of chess," was the most eccentric of the small group of those who, under a bit different circumstances, may have become world champion.

A very difficult personality, he couldn't attract a backer and so lost his opportunity to play Capablanca. (What a conflict of personalities and ideas that would have proven!) Later Alekhine preferred to beat up on Bogolubov several times rather than oppose the "prince."

ROOK VERSUS ROOK AND TWO PAWNS

A rook and two pawns usually—but not always—win against the rook.

KLING AND HORWITZ

Diagram 201
White to move

Here, even though White has two connected, passed pawns, they're blocked. Black manages to draw.

1. Rd4 Rb6

Black has to control the sixth rank.

2. Rd8 Rb4+ 3. Ke5 Rb7!

Black threatens to capture the g5-pawn.

4. Rg8+ Kh7 5. Rd8 Kg6, draw.

SPECIAL CASE OF THE ROOK-
AND BISHOP-PAWNS

The weaker side often reaches a draw against a pair of isolated
pawns on the f- and h-files or the a- and c-files. The main techniques employed in the defense are the long-side defense and
the rook attack from the bottom of the board.

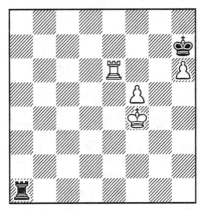

Diagram 202
White to move

1. Kg5

Or 1. Ke5 Re1+ 2. Kf6 Rf1.

1. ... Rg1+ 2. Kf6 Rf1!

Black must prevent 3. Kf7. Capturing with 2. ... Kxh6 is bad
because of 3. Ke7+ Kh7 4. f6 Ra1 5. f7.

3. Re3

If 3. Re5, then 3. ... Kxh6 4. Kf7 Ra1 5. f6 Ra7+ 6. Re7 Ra8 7.
Re8 Ra7+ 8. Ke6 Ra6+ 9. Kf5 Ra5+ 10. Re5 Ra7 11. Ke6
Ra6+, with the draw.

3. ... Ra1 4. Re6

If 4. Kf7, 4. ... Kxh6.

4. ... Rf1, draw.

ROOK AND PAWNS VS. ROOK AND PAWNS

In this next case, Black's rook is in front of the opponent's passed pawn, blocking it. This arrangement significantly restricts the rook's mobility, sometimes leading to zugzwang. If Black's king moves to assist his rook, then his pawns on the other side of the board become vulnerable. Still, in most cases, the weaker side's king should try to block the passed pawn, freeing up his rook for action.

ALEKHINE—CAPABLANCA
BUENOS AIRES, 1927

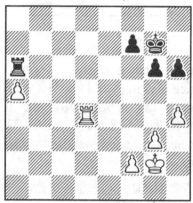

Diagram 203
White to move

1. Ra4

Now White wants to bring his king to attack the Black rook. That's why the Black king should travel to the scene to help.

1. ... Kf6 2. Kf3 Ke5 3. Ke3 h5

This typical move, which tries to prevent g3-g4 and h4-h5, has its negatives here, as it will allow White's king to penetrate via g5.

4. Kd3 Kd5 5. Kc3 Kc5 6. Ra2

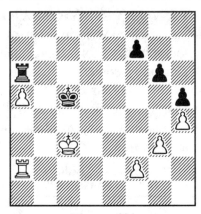

Diagram 204

White waits for his opponent to use up all of his useful moves. Black can't win the a-pawn because it would lead to a losing pawn ending, since his king would be left too far away from the kingside. After 6. ... Ra8, White would play 7. a6, limiting the mobility of the Black rook even more. That's why Black regroups so that his king can block the pawn, freeing his rook for other actions.

6. ... Kb5 7. Kd4!

In the actual game, the two legendary champions played 7. Kb3 Kc5 8. Kc3 Kb5, repeating the position. Then Alekhine went for the win with Kd4!. While Black's king is distracted, White heads to the kingside pawns.

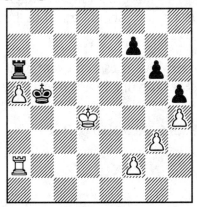

Diagram 205

7. ... Rd6+ 8. Ke5 Re6+ 9. Kf4 Ka6 10. Kg5 Re5+ 11. Kh6 Rf5

Now Alekhine played 12. f4 and eventually won. But the fastest way to win is …

12. Kg7 Rf3 13. Rd2!

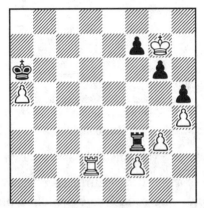

Diagram 206

This is an important moment. White's rook abandons his own passed pawn in favor of attacking the Black pawns, because it's then two-against-one on the kingside. This sets up unstoppable, winning threats: 14. Rd6+ and 15. Rf6. If 13. ... Kxa5, then 14. Rd5+! Kb6 15. Rd6+ and 16. Rf6. Or if 14. ... Kb4, then 15. Rd4+ and 16. Rf4, with the win.

ROOKS NORMALLY BELONG *BEHIND* THE PASSED PAWN—WHETHER IT'S YOURS OR YOUR OPPONENT'S.

ILIVITSKY—KROGIUS
RUSSIA, 1956

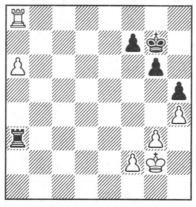

Diagram 207
White to move

Again, White has an extra, distant passed pawn.

However, there is a significant difference between this and the previous example. The rooks have switched places. Here, the Black rook not only guards the passed pawn from the rear, but can also attack White's kingside. White can't count on 1. a7 to win, since then if White's king tries to approach his passed pawn to give support, Black's rook checks from the bottom of the board, driving the enemy king away.

So all of White's hopes reside in temporarily keeping his pawn on a6. By resisting the urge to push the pawn, White leaves the a7-square available to shelter his king from checks. But while White follows this plan, Black's rook can take the White pawns on the other side of the board!

1. Kf1 Ra2 2. Ke1 Kf6 3. f3

3. Kd1 is too risky because of 3. ... Rxf2 4. Kc1 Ra2 5. Kb1 Ra5 6. Kb2 Kf5 7. Kb3 Kg4 8. Kb4 Ra1 9. Kb5 Kxg3.

3. ... Ra3! 4. Ke2 Kg7 5. Kd2 Rxf3

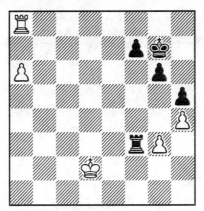

Diagram 208

6. Kc2 Rxg3 7. Kb2 Rg2+ 8. Kb3 Rg1 9. Kb2 Rg2+ 10. Kb3 Rg1

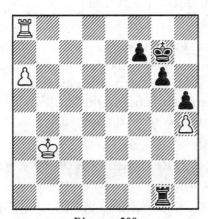

Diagram 209

11. Kb2, draw.

In the case of 11. Kb4, Black can play 11. ... Ra1 12. Kb5 g5! 13. hxg5 h4 14. Rc8 h3 15. Rc2 Kg6 16. Rh2 Ra3, with advantage for Black.

ELISKASES—LEVENFISH
MOSCOW, 1936

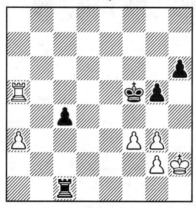

Diagram 210
Black to move

Black, although down a pawn, enjoys two important circumstances in his favor.

  ♟ Black's king is more active;

  ♟ Black's passed pawn is closer to the center, allowing its king to support it. (In this particular position, it is better for Black that his pawn is not so distant. This fact is not typical for most endings, where you normally want the most distant passed pawn.)

1. ... Ke6! 2. Ra6+ Kd5 3. Rxh6 c3 4. Rh8 Ra1 5. Rc8 Rxa3 6. Kh3?

White should play 6. f4, with good chances of drawing.

Diagram 211

6. ... Kd4 7. Kg4

Now if 7. f4, then 7. ... gxf4 8. gxf4 c2+ 9. Kh4 Rc3.

7. ... Ra5 8. f4 Rc5 9. Rd8+ Ke3 10. Rd1 c2 11. Rc1 gxf4 12. gxf4 Kd2 13. Ra1 c1(Q) 14. Rxc1 Rxc1!

The king has to stay close to the pawns.

15. Kg5 Ke3 16. f5 Ke4

Diagram 212

17. g4 Ke5 18. Kg6 Rc6+ 19. Kg7 Ra6! 20. Kf7 Kf4 21. Kg7

If 21. f6, then 21. ... Kg5.

21. ... Kg5, White resigns.

As we've seen, a rook in these endings is usually better off behind, rather than in front of, passed pawns, no matter whose pawns they are. When a rook is guarding a pawn from the side, it can be active on the other side of the board. This freedom for the rook is good. On the other hand, this pawn can't move forward without help from its king.

KROGIUS—GIBBS
OSLO, 1954

Diagram 213
Black to move

White's winning plan is to transfer his king to the queenside. Black's next move makes White's task easier.

1. ... g5?

Now White gets a comfortable station for his rook and an easy win. But even after the best move, 1. ... Rb4, White has a good chance to win after 2. Kf2 Rb3 3. Ke2 Kf6 4. f4, followed by the further advance of the White king.

2. Kf2

On the premature 2. Rf5?, Black draws with 2. ... Rb2!.

2. ... Kf6 3. Ke2 Ke6 4. Rf5 f6 5. Kd2 Ke7 6. Kc2 Rb4

7. Kc3 Rb1 8. Kc4 Rc1+ 9. Kd5, winning.

Connected passed pawns can develop into an unstoppable juggernaut if they cannot be blocked.

BOTVINNIK—KOPILOV
MOSCOW, 1951

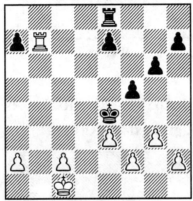

Diagram 214
White to move

1. Rxa7?

The coming connected passed pawns provide Black with more than adequate compensation for the material discrepancy. White had to play 1. Kd2, to meet 1. ... Kf3 with 2. Ke1, and White should hold; for example—2. ... Rc8 3. Rxe7 Rxc2 4. Rxa7 Rxf2 5. Rxh7 Rxa2 6. h4 Kxe3 7. Re7+ Kf3 8. Re6 =.

1. ... Kf3 2. a4 Kxf2 3. a5 g5 4. a6 Kxe3 5. Rb7 e5 6. a7 Ra8

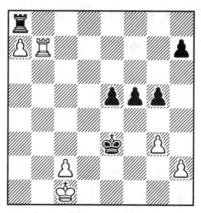

Diagram 215

7. Rxh7

A better try was 7. Rb5 e4 8. Rxf5 Rxa7 9. Rxg5.

7. ... f4 8. gxf4 gxf4 9. Kd1 f3

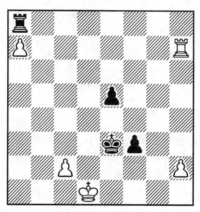

Diagram 216

10. c4

Or 10. Ke1 Rg8 11. Kf1 Rd8 -+.

10. ... Rd8+ 11. Kc2 f2 12. Rf7 Ra8, White resigns.

The threat is 13. ... Rxa7.

BEWARE OF PASSIVE DEFENSE

In these rook endings, passive play is often self-defeating.

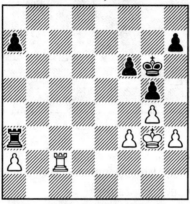

**ILIVITSKY—TAIMANOV
MOSCOW, 1954**

Diagram 217
White to move

1. Rh2?

White had to play 1. Rc6!, activating his rook with a pawn sacrifice; for example— 1. ... Rxa2 2. h4 gxh4+ 3. Kxh4 Ra3 4. Kg3 a5 5. Ra6, with good chances for a draw. This is a typical defensive technique in such endings.

1. ... h5 2. Rc2?

Worth a try 2. h4!?, to get as many pawns off the board as possible, and avoid the terribly passive position White now gets.

2. ... h4+ 3. Kf2 a6 4. Rb2 Rc3 5. Kg2 a5

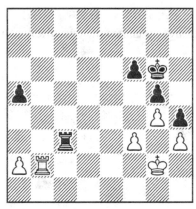

Diagram 218

Now 6. Rb7 Rc2+ 7. Kg1 Rxa2 8. Ra7 would lose because of the bad position of White's pawns, and especially that of his king—cut off on the first rank.

6. Rf2 Ra3 7. Kf1 Kf7

The king is heading to f4.

8. f4 gxf4 9. Rxf4 Kg6 10. Rf2 Rxh3, White resigns.

Let's look at another example where having an active rook trumps material advantage.

IN ROOK ENDINGS, IT'S BETTER TO BE A PAWN DOWN WITH AN ACTIVE ROOK THAN TO HAVE MATERIAL EQUALITY IN A PASSIVE POSITION.

SCHLECHTER—EM. LASKER
VIENNA, MATCH GAME #1, 1910

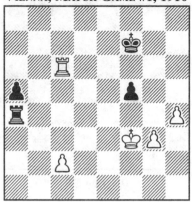

Diagram 219
Black to move

1. ... Re4!

Despite being a pawn down, Black's active pieces allow him to hold by sacrificing another pawn! Weaker is the obvious 1. ... Ra1, as after 2. Ra6 a4 3. Kf4 Rf1+ 4. Ke5 Rf3 5. Rxa4 Rxg3 6. Rf4 Kg6 7. Rxf5 Rc3 8. Rf2, White is winning, although he has a difficult technical task.

2. Rc5 Kf6 3. Rxa5 Rc4

In the actual game, Schlechter repeated the position by checking Lasker's king back and forth a few times with Ra6 and Ra5. Then he decided to hold his c-pawn.

4. Ra2 Rc3+ 5. Kg2 Ke5

Diagram 220

White has two extra pawns, but his pieces are tied up.

6. Rb2 Kf6 7. Kh3 Rc6 8. Rb8

Giving away a pawn, but there is nothing better.

8. ... Rxc2

As is most often the case, this ending with the two pawns against one on the same side is a draw.

9. Rb6+ Kg7 10. h5 Rc4

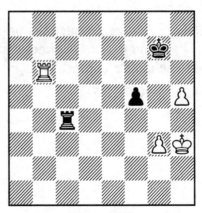

Diagram 221

11. h6+ Kh7 12. Rf6 Ra4, draw.

TARRASCH—RUBINSTEIN
SAN SEBASTIAN, 1911

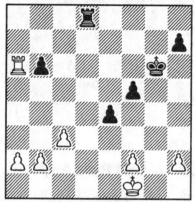

Diagram 222
Black to move

By activating his pieces, Black can reach a draw in a position that at first glance seems hopeless.

1. ... Rd2!

1. ... Rd6? 2. Ke1 and 3. a4.

2. Rxb6+ Kg5 3. Ke1

Or 3. a4 f4 4. a5 f3 5. Ke1 Re2+ =. A rook on the seventh rank is a force to contend with in most positions, endgame or not.

3. ... Rc2 4. Rb5 Kg4

Diagram 223

With the idea of 5. ... f4 and 6. ... f3 or 6. ... Kf3.

5. h3+ Kxh3 6. Rxf5 Rxb2 7. Rf4

Or 7. a4 Ra2 8. a5 Kg4 9. Re5 Kf3 10. Rf5+ Kg4 =.

7. ... Rxa2 8. Rxe4 h5 9. c4 Kg2 10. Rf4 Rc2 11. Rh4 Kf3! 12. Kd1 Rxf2 13. c5 Ke3 14. Rxh5 Kd4, draw.

SAVON—ZELIANDINOV
RIGA, 1964

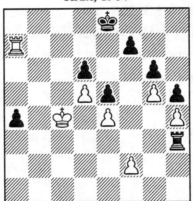

Diagram 224
White to move

His king's active position fully compensates White for his missing pawn.

1. Kb5 Rxh4?

Black had to think draw, not win. After 1. ... Rc3! (cutting off White's king) 2. Rxa4 Rc2 3. Ra7 Rc1 4. Kb6 Rc2 5. Rc7 Ra2! 6. Kc6 Ra6+ 7. Kb5 Ra2, Black would draw.

2. Kc6 Rxe4 3. Kxd6 Kf8 4. Ra8+ Kg7 5. Ke7

Black's pawns protect the White king against checks from the bottom of the board.

Diagram 225

5. ... Rd4 6. d6 e4

Or 6. ... h4 7. d7 h3 8. d8Q Rxd8 9. Rxd8 h2 10. Rd1 a3 11. Rh1 a2 12. Ra1 e4 13. Rh1 Kg8 14. Kf6 Kf8 15. Ke5, with a win.

7. d7 e3 8. fxe3 Re4+ 9. Kd6 Rxe3 10. d8(Q), Black resigns.

We've seen that in rook endings an extra pawn doesn't guarantee a win. These endings are especially drawish when the pawns are on the same side of the board. Thus, positions with two pawns versus one, three versus two, or even four pawns versus three—all on one side of the board—are drawn in most cases. As in pawn endings, the more pawns, the more chances the superior side has to create a passed pawn and win. For his part, the defending side should trade off as many pawns as he can.

RAZUVAEV—BELIAVSKY
MOSCOW, 1978

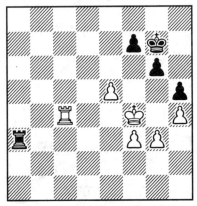

Diagram 226
White to move

1. g4

Or 1. Ke4 Rb3 2. Rd4 Ra3 3. Rd3 Ra4+ 4. Ke3 Ra5.

1. ... hxg4 2. Kxg4

If 2. fxg4 Black easily holds with 2. ... Ra1!, but not 2. ... Rh3 3. e6! fxe6 4. Rc7+ Kf8 5. Kg5 Rg3 6. Kf6 +-.

2. ... Ra1 3. Rc7 Rg1+ 4. Kf4 Re1! 5. Ra7 Re2 6. Ra1 Rg2 7. Re1 Kf8 8. h5 gxh5 9. Rh1 f6 10. Rxh5

10. e6 Rg5.

10. ... fxe5+ 11. Rxe5 Ra2 12. Kf5, draw agreed.

THE WEAKER SIDE SHOULD TRY TO
ACHIEVE A POSITION WITH PAWNS
ON ONLY ONE SIDE OF THE BOARD.

Summary: *Rook endings account for half the endgames you're likely to reach. Reviewing this chapter regularly, along with the first three chapters, will lead to more and more endgame wins. (Remember, opening variations come and go, but winning endgame technique is always in fashion!) Next to bishop-of-opposite-color endings, rook endings are the most drawish. As in most other endings, the defending king should try to get in front of the passed pawn(s). Rooks generally belong behind passed pawns, whether the pawn is yours or your opponent's.*

When rook and one pawn opposes rook, the rook pawn is, as usual, the most likely to lead to a draw. Passive defense, where the defender's rook stays on the back rank, holding down the fortress, succeeds against knight- and rook-pawns. Philidor's position is an important one to remember, and once reached, leads to an easy draw. When Philidor's position is unreachable, the defender still has effective techniques to fight for a draw. The long-side defense can lead to a draw, if the rook has enough lateral room to operate. When the defending side's king is cut off from the queening path of the pawn, using his rook to attack frontally is often the only successful defense. On the other hand, the Lucena position is a basic winning technique in which the superior side "builds a bridge" to shelter his king from checks and promote his pawn. Rook and two pawns usually win against the lone rook, except for the special case of rook-and bishop-pawns.

When both sides have pawns, remember that it's better to be down a pawn and have an active rook, than to be even materially and suffer the disadvantage of a passive position. When one side is up a pawn, the more pawns on the board, the more likely the win. In such cases the stronger side should try to keep pawns on the board in order to maximize chances of creating a passed pawn, while the defender should try to exchange as many pawns as possible. After all, if a game boils down to a one-pawn advantage, with all pawns on the same side of the board, it's usually a draw.

Rook Endings
Learning Exercises

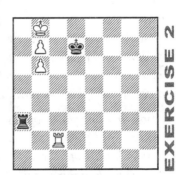

Diagram 227
White to move

Diagram 228
White to move

Diagram 229
White to move

Diagram 230
White to move

Diagram 231
Black to move

Diagram 232
White to move

Rook Endings
Solutions

No. 1   **1. Rb7 Rxb5 2. Kg6 Kf8 3. h6 Re5 4. Rb8+ +-.**

No. 2   **1. Rd2+ Ke7 2. Rd6 Rc3** (2. ... Kxd6 3. Kc8 Rc3+ 4. Kd8) **3. Rc6 Rxc6 4. Ka7 +-.**

No. 3   **1. e5 fxe5** (1. ... Rxe5+ 2. Kc6 or 1. ... Rd2+ 2. Ke6) **2. Ke6 Rc2 3. Ra8+ Rc8 4. Rxc8+ Kxc8 5. Ke7 +-.**

No. 4   **1. f5 exf5 2. Kf4 Re6 3. Kxf5 Rg6**
(3. ... Kf7 4. Rg3 Rh6 5. Rg5 Rh7 6. Rg6 +-) **4. e6 Rg4 5. Ke5 Re4+ 6. Kd6 Rxd4** (6. ... Kf8 7. Kd7) **7. Re3 +-.**

No. 5   **1. ... Ke4! 2. b7 f5 3. b8(Q) Rxb8 4. Rxb8 f4 5. Rb1 f3 6. Kc5 f2 =** (not 1. ... Kg4? 2. b7 f5 3. b8(Q) Rxb8 4. Rxb8 f4 5. Kd5 f3 6. Ke4 f2 7. Rf8 Kg3 8. Ke3 +-).

No. 6   **1. Ra1 Ke6** (1. ... Rb2+ 2. Kc5 Rb8 3. Kd6 +-)
2. Rd1 Rb2+ 3. Ka5! (3. Kc5 Rb8) **3. ... Rb8 4. c5 Ke7 5. c6 Rd8 6. Rxd8 Kxd8 7. Kb6 +-.**

Chapter 5: Knight Endings
Some Important Ideas to Look For

◆ The knight and pawn protect each other.

See Diagram 235.

◆ The knight deflects the enemy cavalry to queen the pawn.

Black has just played 10. ... Nf4. See Diagram 239.

◆ The White knight spears the new queen with a fork.

White has just played 15. Ne3+. See Diagram 245.

◆ Knight and pawn stop two pawns.

White has just played 15. Nc6. See Diagram 256.

Chapter 5
Knight Endings:
Springer of Surprises

Many of the "magical" moments created on the chessboard involve the game's only jumpers. Indeed, German players call the knight a "Springer." Knights are the obvious odd-men-out of the chess board, with a short-hopping, non-linear way of moving all their own—a far cry from the straight-line, ground-hugging travel of the other pieces. Naturally, this difference leads to positions and principles unique to the knight.

To get ourselves oriented, let's look at several famous positions.

Diagram 233
White to move

Despite his significant material advantage, White can't win. If he sends his king to support the pawn, when his monarch reaches a6 or b6 he achieves only stalemate, with Black's king tucked, tortoise-like, into the corner.

❖ ❖ ♔ ❖ ❖

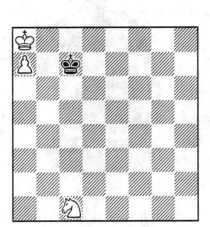

Diagram 234
White to move

The play in this position is even more paradoxical than in the last. If it's White's move, his knight is not able to force the release of his blockaded king.

1. Nd3 Kc8 2. Nc5 Kc7 3. Ne6+

A check here is a good omen for the defender.

3. ... Kc8 4. Nd4 Kc7 5. Nb5+

It's a draw in all variations. But with Black on move, the result is quite different.

1. ... Kc8 2. Nd3 Kc7 3. Nc5 Kc8 4. Ne6 Kd7 5. Kb7

White is winning.

Analyzing Diagram 234 shows us a unique limitation of the knight, caused by its singular way of moving. In such a position, the knight can't lose or "pass" the move in the way other pieces often can. For example, in Chapter 2, we've seen how the king can triangulate to "hand back a position" in the pawn endings.

WITH THE STRONGER SIDE ON MOVE, WHEN HIS KNIGHT AND OPPONENT'S KING ARE ON SQUARES OF THE SAME COLOR, IT IS A DRAW. WITH THE SAME CONDITIONS, BUT THE KNIGHT AND KING ON DIFFERENT COLORS, THE STRONGER SIDE WINS.

Diagram 235
White or Black to move

Here we see a typical example of a "mutual defense pact" between knight and passed pawn. This deployment of a knight and pawn is often the result of a successful endgame strategy. In this example, White has an easy win. First of all, he uses his king to capture the Black pawn on g7. Then he forces the promotion of his own passed pawn. Were the knight ahead of the pawn—say, on a6 or b7—the game would quickly end in a draw.

KNIGHT AND PAWN AGAINST KNIGHT

Let's look at two masters plying their craft in the most basic knight ending. In positions with knight and pawn against knight, with the weaker side's king far away, all that's required for the stronger side to win is pushing the opponent's knight out of the way of the passed pawn. The king and knight must usually work together to achieve this goal.

PETROV—ARONIN
RUSSIA, 1950

Diagram 236
White to move

White's defense is difficult because of his king's bad position, cut off from the path of his opponent's pawn.

1. Ne3 g3 2. Ng2 Nf5

Black limits the movement of White's knight and prepares to relocate his king to f3.

3. Kc4 Ke4 4. Kc3 Kf3 5. Ne1+ Ke2

Some knights don't leap,
they limp.
—Tartakover

Diagram 237

6. Ng2

White's 6. Nd3 loses because of ... Ke3 7. Ne1 Nh4 8. Kc2 Ke2 9. Nd3 Ng6 10. Nc1+ Ke3.

6. ... Kf1 7. Nf4 Ne7!

Black threatens 8. ... Ng6.

8. Kd2 Ng6

Diagram 238

9. Nh3

White can't be decoyed by capturing Black's Trojan horse, because the pawn would then march to his final goal unopposed. If White plays 9. Ne2, then 9. ... g2 10. Ke3 Nf4!, and we would get the following position.

Diagram 239
After 10. ... Nf4!

Once again, Black would be delighted to sacrifice his knight in order to distract the opponent's forces from the pawn. This kind of tactical punch is typical of positions with a knight and pawn against a lone knight. Back to the game.

    9. ... g2
    10. Ke3 Ne5!

It is not a move, even the best move, that you seek,
but a realizable plan.
            —*Znosko-Borovsky*

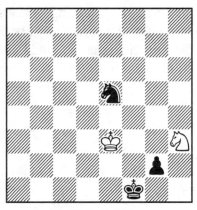

Diagram 240
White to move

White resigns because there is no defense to Black's knight reaching f2—for example, 11. Kf4 Nd3+ 12. Kg3 Nf2.

❖ ❖ ♔ ❖ ❖

Siegbert Tarrasch (1862-1934) was perhaps the strongest player never to be world champion. Brilliant, arrogant, dogmatic and caustically witty, he was the first great chess writer-teacher.

He valued mobility above all other positional considerations. A physician, he wrote memorably: "Cramped positions bear the germs of defeat."

Courtesy www.chesscafe.com

THE KING TAKES PART IN THE DEFENSE

BENKO—BRONSTEIN
BUDAPEST, 1949

Diagram 241
White to move

Here the defender's king is playing an active role in the defense, allowing White to reach a draw. In fact, in the actual game, the players agreed to a draw in this position. Let's see why.

1. Ne4 Ng4

There's an instant draw after 1. ... Nf1 2. Ng5 f2 3. Ne4 and 4. Nxf2.

2. Kd2 Ne5

If 2. ... Nf6, then 3. Nxf6 f2 4. Ng4 f1(Q) 5. Ne3+, with a draw.

3. Ke3 Nc4+ 4. Kd4

When you don't know what to do, wait for your opponent
to get an idea, it's sure to be wrong!
—Siegbert Tarrasch

Diagram 242

4. ... Na3

Or 4. ... Nd6 5. Nxd6! f2 6. Nf5 and 7. Ne3+.

5. Kd3 Nb5 6. Kd2 Nd4 7. Kd3 Ne6

With the threat 8. ... Nc5+.

8. Ke3

Diagram 243

8. ... Nc7

If 8. ... Nc5, then 9. Nf2!.

9. Kd3 Nd5 10. Kc2 Ne3+ 11. Kc3 Nf5 12. Kd2 Ng3

Three-time World Champion

First of the long line of Soviet World Champions

◆ Popularizer of the "scientific approach"

◆ Pioneer in computer chess research

◆ Endgame wizard who studied the game's final stage throughout his career

◆ By his own description, "First among equals."

Master of the Endgame
Mikhail Botvinnik

Place of Birth: St. Petersburg
Date of Birth: August 17, 1911

Mikhail Botvinnik was world champion three different times. After Alexander Alekhine died while still champion, Botvinnik won the special FIDE tournament that pitted the world's top five players—Botvinnik, Keres, Reshevsky, Smyslov, and Euwe—against one another for the title. Botvinnik dominated the event, thus becoming the sixth to hold the world title— and first in the long line of Soviet world champions.

Like Lasker, Botvinnik was both a great defender and an unsurpassed endgame player. He was well known for his disciplined training procedures, which included a devotion to studying the endgame.

Although Botvinnik did not have the impressive tournament results of some reigning world champions, he did have an iron will and an ability to regroup. In 1957 he lost to Smyslov and then won a rematch in 1958. He followed the same pattern with Mikhail Tal in 1960 and 1961. Finally, in 1963 he lost his title to Tigran Petrosian. Since by that time Botvinnik did not have the right to an automatic rematch, he declined to go for a fourth term. He died in 1995.

Diagram 244

All Black's attempts to push his opponent's pieces out of the way have failed.

13. Nf6 f2 14. Ng4 f1(Q) 15. Ne3+, draw.

Diagram 245

DISTANT PASSED PAWNS ARE QUITE
IMPORTANT AND PLAY THE SAME ROLE
WE'RE NOW USED TO, DIVERSION.
THE WINNING PLAN USUALLY INVOLVES
THE SUPERIOR KING'S
GETTING TO HIS OPPONENT'S
DEFENSELESS PAWNS.

BOTH SIDES HAVE PAWNS, AND ONE IS PASSED

In knight endings with passed pawns, the principles of play are very similar to those in pawn endings.

SCHMIDT—KASPAROV
DUBAI, 1986

Diagram 246
Black to move

Besides his distant passed pawn, Black has another advantage—the better placed king.

1. ... Ke7 2. Nc4 a4 3. Kf1 Ke6 4. Ke2 Kd5

Diagram 247

5. Ne3+

If 5. Na3, then 5. ... Ne5 (with the threat of 6. ... Nc4); 5. Kd3 loses because of 5. ... Ne5+, when Black makes the transition to a winning pawn ending.

5. ... Kd4 6. Kd2 Ne5 7. Kc2 Nd3 8. Nd1 Ne1+ 9. Kb2 Nf3 10. h4

Diagram 248

10. ... Ne5!

This is more accurate than 10. ... Kd3, because then White could try 11. Ne3 Ke2 12. h5 gxh5 13. Nd5, when he would have some slight tactical counter chances with 14. Nf6. Kasparov obviously prefers not to give any such opportunities to his opponent.

11. Ka3 Ke4 12. h5

Otherwise, Black would have played h7-h5, Kf3 and Ng4. But White can't head off the ultimate outcome.

12. ... gxh5 13. Ne3 Kf3

Diagram 249

Black's strategy triumphs.

14. Nd5 Ng4!

Illuminating the "no vacancy" sign on f6 for the White knight.

15. Ne7

If 15. Nf4, then 15. ... Nf6 16. Nd3 Ke2.

15. ... Nxf2 16. Nf5 Ne4 17. Kxa4 Nxg3 18. Nh4+ Ke4 19. Kb4 Nf5, White resigns.

WING MAJORITIES

RABINOVICH—BELAVENETS
TBILISI, 1937

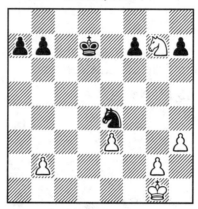

Diagram 250
White to move

In Diagram 250, White has an extra pawn on the kingside. Black has an extra pawn on the queenside. But it is easier for Black to create a passed pawn because:

- Having two pawns against one is ideal for creating a passed pawn.
- It is difficult for White to create counter chances on the kingside, because he has a less favorable pawn majority (three against two) and his pawns are poorly placed for the job. Additionally, his isolated pawn on e3 is blocked by Black's knight.
- Black's pieces have more active positions. They dominate the center and are ready for action on either side.

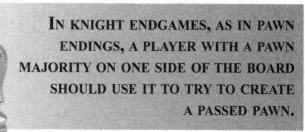

IN KNIGHT ENDGAMES, AS IN PAWN
ENDINGS, A PLAYER WITH A PAWN
MAJORITY ON ONE SIDE OF THE BOARD
SHOULD USE IT TO TRY TO CREATE
A PASSED PAWN.

Considering all of these factors, we can judge this position as much better, perhaps even winning, for Black.

1. Kf1 Kc6 2. Ke2 Kd5 3. Nf5 Kc4 4. Nd4 a5 5. h4 a4 6. g4 b5

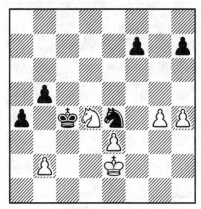

Diagram 251

7. Kd1

Admitting defeat. But Black also wins after 7. g5 b4 8. Kd1 Kd3 9. Nf5 b3.

7. ... Nf2+ 8. Kc2 Nxg4 9. Nf5 f6, White resigns.

White's position is hopeless after 10. Nd6+ Kb4 11. e4 Kc5 12. Nb7+ Kd4 13. Nd6 b4.

Garry Kasparov (1963-) became 13th World Champion in 1985 by defeating Anatoly Karpov, who had been ceded the title when Bobby Fischer refused to defend his crown. Kasparov later broke with FIDE (the World Chess Federation).

These events severed the direct connection to the century-old line of world champions tracing their legitimacy to Steinitz.

Photo by Bill Hook, Courtesy USCF

IMPORTANCE OF THE ACTIVE KING

The following example shows how to make the most of an active king in knight and pawn endings.

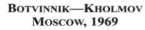

Diagram 252
Black to move

White's king is more active, and this factor is decisive.

1. ... Kc7 2. Ng5 f6 3. Nh7 f5

Black would make it worse for himself with 3. ... Ng8, because of 4. Kd5 Kd7 5. Nf8+ and 6. Nxg6.

4. h4

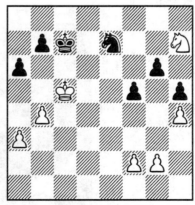

Diagram 253

4. ... f4

Actually forced, because of 4. ... b6+ 5. Kd4 Kd6 6. Nf8 Nc6+ 7. Ke3 Ne5 8. Kf4, when the White king breaks through to the pawns.

5. Nf8 b6+ 6. Kd4 Nf5+ 7. Ke4 Nxh4 8. Ne6+! Kc6 9. Nxf4

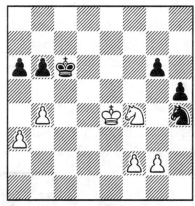

Diagram 254

9. ... Kb5

In case of 9. ... g5 10. g3 gxf4 11. gxh4, White would have an easy win in the pawn ending.

10. g3 Nf5 11. Nxg6 Nh6

Or 11. ... Nd6+ 12. Kd5 Nc4 13. f4 Nxa3 14. f5 +-.

12. Ne5! Ka4 13. Nc4

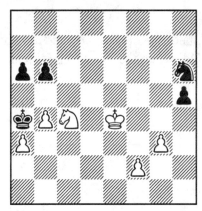

Diagram 255

13. ... Kb3

After the obvious 13. ... b5, White would use the following important technique: 14. Na5 Kxa3 15. Nc6.

Diagram 256
After 15. Nc6

White has immunity on the queenside (15. ... a5 16. bxa5 b4 17. a6 or 15. ... Kb3 16. Kf4 Kc4 17. Kg5 Nf7+ 18. Kxh5 Kd5 19. Na5), while on the other side of the board, White's king supports his pawns in their quest for promotion.

14. Nxb6 Kxa3 15. Nd5

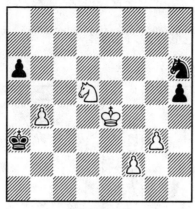

Diagram 257

15. ... Kb3 16. Nc7 Kxb4 17. Nxa6+, Black resigns.

If 17. ... Kb5 18. Nc7+ Kc6 19. Ne6 Nf7 20. Ng7 Ng5+ 21. Ke3+-.

Summary: *The knight has unique characteristics—it's the only "jumper" on the chessboard, and it's the only piece that doesn't move in a straight line. So it is often the "springer of surprises." Not surprisingly, play with the knight is guided by special principles. For example, a lone king facing king, knight, and a rook pawn on the seventh rank can draw fairly easily by blocking the opponent's king to the corner if, with the attacker to move, the defender's king and knight are on the same color squares. When king, knight and pawn oppose king and knight, the superior side can frequently offer to sacrifice his knight to decoy the defender's knight from the passed pawn. The superior side can usually win if his king and knight can work together to push the defending knight out of the path of the passed pawn while the defender's king is far enough away. As in pawn endings, a player with a majority of pawns on one side of the board should use this superiority to try to produce a passed pawn, which can then be used to divert the defender's pieces.*

Knight Endings
Learning Exercises

Diagram 258
White to move

Diagram 259
White to move

Diagram 260
Black to move

Diagram 261
White to move

Diagram 262
Black to move

Diagram 263
Black to move

EXERCISE 1

EXERCISE 2

EXERCISE 3

EXERCISE 4

EXERCISE 5

EXERCISE 6

Knight Endings
Solutions

No. 1   **1. e6 Nc5+ 2. Ke2 Nxe6 3. Kf1 h2 4. Ne2+ Kf3 5. Ng1+ Kg3 6. Ne2+ =.**

No. 2   **1. Nd6+ Kd8** (1. ... Ke7 2. Ne4 Na6 3. Nf6 h6 4. Ng8+ +-) **2. Nb7+ Nxb7 3. a6 Kc7 4. a7 +-.**

No. 3   **1. ... Nc3 2. bxc3 a4 3. cxd4 cxd4 4. c3 a3 -+.**

No. 4   **1. f6 gxf6 2. h5 Nxg3 3. h6 Nf5 4. h7 Nd6+ 5. Kb4 Nf7 6. Ne6** (threatening 7. Nc5#) **6. ... Kb7 7. Nd8+ +-.**

No. 5   **1. ... Nxg7 2. Nxg7 c4 3. cxb4 cxb3 4. Kd1 e3 -+.**

No. 6   **1. ... Nd3 2. Ke2** (2. Kxd3 h3 3. Ne3 Kf4 4. Nf1 Kxf3 -+) **2. ... Nf4+ 3. Nxf4 gxf4 4. Kf2 Kd4 5. Kg2 Kc3 6. Kh3 Kb2 -+.**

Chapter 6: Bishop Endings
Some Important Ideas to Look For

◆White's bad bishop allows Black to draw.

Black plays 1. ... Be7.
See Diagram 273.

◆ An impregnable fortress
No matter who moves, Black draws.

See Diagram 290.

◆White wins because his pawns are far apart and far advanced.

See Diagram 314.

◆ White's good bishop gives him the win.

See Diagram 279.

Chapter 6
Bishop Endings:
Diagonal Dexterity

At the beginning of the game, and as long as they remain on the board, your bishop pair live in separate, parallel universes. They slide by each other obliquely, a team of doppelgänger who can never make mutual contact. A pair of bishops on the relatively open board of an endgame can catch an opponent in the equivalent of machine-gun cross-fire. A single, unobstructed bishop in an endgame remains speedier than a knight springing from one edge of the board to the other. But unlike the knight, the bishop serves with the severe limitation of being unable to contact 32 of the 64 squares. Half the real estate is off limits.

Endings take on a very different character depending on whether the opposing bishops move on the same or opposite-color squares. We'll first look at the battle of same-color bishops.

PART 1: BISHOPS OF THE SAME COLOR

Here the opposing bishops can make head-to-head contact. For instance, there is the chance that the stronger side can block the defending bishop from being able to give itself for a single, dangerous passed pawn. Clearly, these same-color-bishop endings are less drawish than endings where the opposing bishops travel on differently colored squares.

PAWN ON THE SIXTH OR SEVENTH RANK

To get our bearings, let's look at some positions where a lone bishop opposes another bishop and a pawn on the sixth or seventh rank (where it has only one crucial square to cross before queening), with the stronger side's king positioned ahead of the pawn.

CHENTURINI

Diagram 264
White to move

It's obvious that since neither side can mate the other with a lone bishop and his king, White's only threat to win is promotion of his pawn. If Black has any opportunity to sacrifice his bishop for the pawn, the game is immediately drawn. White can't nullify the control of his opponent's bishop over e8 and therefore can't win.

1. Be8 Bd3 2. Bh5 Bb5, draw.

Or 1. Bd3 Bh5 2. Bc2 Bf7 3. Bd1 Bg6, equal.

The famous researcher and cataloger of such positions, Chenturini, observed that the weaker side's bishop must control the square in front of the pawn from one of the two diagonals crossing that square. These two diagonals are never made up of the same number of squares, so Chenturini called them the long and short diagonals. After the defending bishop is pushed from the long diagonal, it has to move to the short one. The outcome of the game depends on the fight for that short diagonal. To draw, the defender's bishop must always have an available move on the short diagonal, so that his king isn't forced to move.

So the fight can center on the defender's "controlled squares," squares that can be safely occupied by his bishop. In Diagram 264, Black controlled two squares on the short diagonal (h5-e8)—including the square it safely occupies, g6. After 1. Be2 he can play 1. ... Bf7, as that square is under his control because of the good position of Black's king, which vertically opposes its White counterpart. If Black's king were someplace else—for example, in diagonal opposition on d6—White would win easily after 1. Bc4 Bh5 2. Bf7, taking control of the diagonal *without occupying the square in front of his pawn*, thus ensuring its promotion.

IF THE WEAKER SIDE CANNOT BE FORCED BY ZUGZWANG TO LEAVE THE SHORT DIAGONAL, HE CAN DRAW. OTHERWISE, HE LOSES.

KLING AND HORWITZ

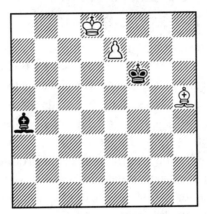

Diagram 265
Black to move

Black can split the point by immediately moving his King to capture the vertical opposition, thus ensuring control of the crucial d7-square.

1. ... Ke5!

1. ... Ke6? 2. Be8 Bd1 3. Bd7+.

2. Bg4

2. Be8 Bd1 3. Bd7 Bh5 =.

2. ... Kd6, draw.

PAWN NOT YET ON THE SIXTH OR SEVENTH RANK

Capturing the vertical opposition from the "bottom" also works in positions where the pawn has not reached the sixth rank and thus has more than one crucial bridge to cross. The defender's goal is to reach the safe formation discussed above.

TAIMANOV—FISCHER
BUENOS AIRES, 1960

Diagram 266
Black to move

Black's 1. ... Kf5 is pretty obvious in this position with an attempt to get into the Berger's Square and in the pawn's way. But this can't be accomplished. After 2. Kd5, b4-b5, and Kc6, White transfers his bishop to the a5-d8 diagonal, and advances his b-pawn. Black's king is shut out. So once again Black needs to get vertical opposition from the "bottom."

1. ... Kf4! 2. b5

2. Kd5 Ke3!

2. ... Ke4 3. Bd4 Bc7 4. Kc5 Kd3 5. Kc6 Kc4

Diagram 267

6. Bb6 Bg3 7. Ba7 Bc7!, draw.

It is not hard to conclude from Chenturini's rule that side pawns are more dangerous than central ones, because of the shortened diagonal side pawns provide to the defending bishop. With a knight-pawn on seventh rank, where the short diagonal has only two squares, the defender can't save himself, even with vertical opposition.

CHENTURINI

Diagram 268
White to move

1. Bh4

To win, White should first take the long diagonal under control, and then deflect his opponent's bishop from the very short a7-b8 diagonal. Here's his winning plan if Black simply waits:

1. ... Bf4 2. Bf2 Bh2 3. Ba7 Bg3 4. Bb8 Bf2 5. Bh2 Ba7 6. Bg1.

Diagram 269
After 6. Bg1

This last move "distracts" or decoys Black's bishop away from his last lane of defense to the queening square. If Black doesn't stop this plan, White wins easily.

Back to Diagram 268. Black, by controlling the a7-square, plays to prevent White's maneuver.

1. ... Kb5 2. Bf2 Ka6 3. Bc5!

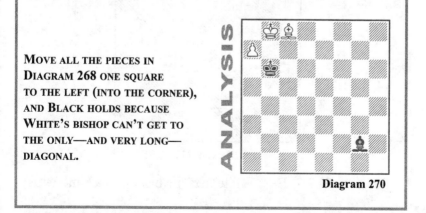

MOVE ALL THE PIECES IN DIAGRAM 268 ONE SQUARE TO THE LEFT (INTO THE CORNER), AND BLACK HOLDS BECAUSE WHITE'S BISHOP CAN'T GET TO THE ONLY—AND VERY LONG—DIAGONAL.

Diagram 270

Diagram 271

Black is in zugzwang. His bishop has to leave the safe haven of h2.

3. ... Bf4 4. Be7 Kb5

White threatens to bring his bishop to c7, so the Black king must rush back to c6.

5. Bd8 Kc6 6. Bg5

Another "distracting" maneuver, 6. Bg5 wins a decisive tempo, confirming the importance of the tempo-passing 3. Bc5.

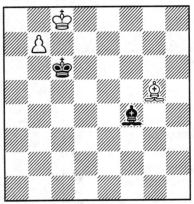

Diagram 272

After 6. ... Bh2 7. Be3, White gets his bishop to a7 and wins.

WITH A KNIGHT-PAWN ON THE SEVENTH RANK, WHERE THE SHORT DIAGONAL HAS ONLY TWO SQUARES, THE WEAKER SIDE CAN'T SAVE HIMSELF, EVEN WITH VERTICAL OPPOSITION.

BISHOP AND TWO PAWNS AGAINST BISHOP

With a bishop and two pawns against bishop, the stronger side usually wins fairly easily. Still there are some drawish positions.

Diagram 273
Black to move

1. ... Be7

White can't strengthen his position because his c-pawn requires protection. For example: 2. e5 Bf8 3. e6 (3. Kd3 Kd5 4. Bd4 Bxc5 5. Bxc5 Kxe5) 3. ... Be7, with a draw.

Two connected passers usually win, but there are complications when the pawns are at the edge of the board, while at the same time the bishop can't control the corner queening square. The defender tries to dissolve the game to the following, key position, a cornerstone in the knowledge of these endings.

Diagram 274
White or Black to move

A snapshot of frustration. Despite White's material superiority, this position is a draw because White can't push Black's king out of the corner. All attempts lead to a stalemate. Yet another illustration of the drawing potential of the rook's pawns when the defender's king is well placed.

❖ ❖ ♚ ❖ ❖

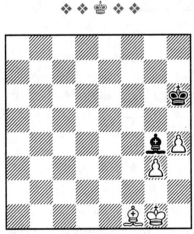

Diagram 275
White to move

Here Black's defense is based on the hope of giving up his bishop for the g-pawn and reaching the drawn position we've just seen in Diagram 274. However, White wins by being wary of that possibility.

1. Kf2 Be6 2. Ke3 Bg4 3. Kf4 Bd7 4. Bd3 Bh3 5. Bf5

White pushes the bishop out from the diagonal h3-c8.

5. ... Bf1 6. g4 Be2 7. g5+ Kh5

Or 7. ... Kg7 8. Bg4 and 9. h5.

Diagram 276

8. Kg3!

If 8. g6? Kh6 9. Ke5 Bh5 10. Kf6 Bxg6 =.

8. ... Bd1 9. Be4 Bb3 10. Bf3+ Kg6 11. Kf4 Bf7
12. h5+ Kg7 13. Ke5 Bb3

13. ... Be8 14. h6+ Kg6 15. Bh5+!.

14. Be4 Bf7 15. h6+ Kh8 16. Kf6 Bh5 17. Bd5 Kh7 18.
Bf7, winning.

White forces Black's bishop off the critical diagonal. The pawn queens. (See diagram on the next page.)

Diagram 277

BOTH SIDES HAVE PAWNS—
THE "BAD" BISHOP

When each side has several pawns, their location is very important. If a player's own pawns are on the same color squares as his bishop, the bishop's mobility is greatly decreased. Thus a bishop can often turn into a "big pawn" and is called a "bad" bishop. When one side has a bad bishop, his opponent's king can frequently penetrate by traveling on squares of the opposite color. When this happens, the defense often fails to a zugzwang position.

Diagram 278
White to move

Here Black has a typically "bad" bishop, passive and limited by its own pawns. White wins if his king can penetrate through e5 or c5 into his opponent's camp. For now Black's king controls those squares, but to remain in control, it has to stand still. Black can thus move only his bishop. Logic dictates that White work to fully restrict this bishop's mobility, so that Black must move his king from the key defensive square of d6. For example, White can meet Black's … Bd7, with Bd3, creating zugzwang and winning. Whether Black moves his king or bishop, he loses critical material.

White has a secondary plan: exchange the queenside pawns and penetrate with his bishop through the a4-e8 diagonal.

1. h4 Be8

If 1. … gxh3 e.p., White forces the zugzwang position we've seen: 2. Bxh3 Bd7 3. Bg2 Be6 (3. … Bc6 4. Bf3) 4. Bf1 Bd7 5. Bd3.

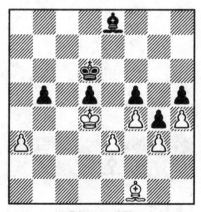

Diagram 279

2. Be2 Bc6

The only move. The d7-square is forbidden fruit for the bishop.

3. Bd1! Bd7

Forced, because 3. … Be8 is bad because of 4. Bc2 Bd7 5. Bd3, or 4. … Bg6 5. Bd3.

4. Bb3 Be6 5. Bc2 Bc8

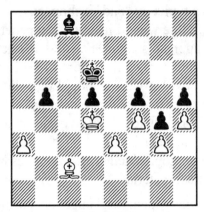

Diagram 280

Now White's "Plan B" is put into action.

6. a4! bxa4

Or 6. ... b4 7. a5 Be6 8. Ba4 Bc8 9. Be8.

7. Bxa4 Be6 8. Be8 Bg8 9. Bxh5, winning.

KASHLEV—ZAGORIANSKY
MOSCOW, 1949

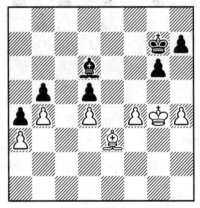

Diagram 281
White to move

After ... Kf6, ... h5+, and ... Kf5, Black is threatening to create a position with the following three threats:

- ♚ attack on the h4-pawn;
- ♚ the sacrifice ... Bxb4, followed by ... a4-a3; and
- ♚ zugzwang, followed by penetration by Black's king with ... Kf5-e4. White tries to prevent his opponent's ominous plans.

1. f5

If White tried 1. h5, then after 1. ... gxh5+ 2. Kxh5 Kf6! 3. Kg4 h5+ 4. Kxh5 Kf5, he would be lost.

1. ... h5+ 2. Kg5 Be7+ 3. Kf4 Kf6! 4. fxg6 Bd6+ 5. Kf3 Kxg6 6. Bf4

Or 6. Bg5 Kf5 7. Be3 Be7 8. Bf2 Bf6 (zugzwang) -+.

6. ... Be7 7. Bg3 Bf6 8. Bf2 Kf5

Diagram 282

Zugzwang! White resigns because he either loses a pawn or lets Black's king penetrate.

BOTH SIDES HAVE PAWNS—THE "GOOD" BISHOP

The "good" bishop is not limited by its own pawns, or tied to their defense. Such a bishop can be very useful in pressing one's advantage as well as in defending.

LILIENTHAL—TOLUSH
PARNU, 1947

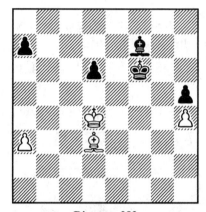

Diagram 283
Black to move

Despite the extra pawn, Black can't win because he's not able to penetrate White's position with his king. The well positioned White pieces create an insurmountable barrier.

1. ... Bg6 2. Bc4 Bf5

2. ... Kf5 3. Bd3+ Kf6 4. Bc4.

   3. Be2 Bg4 4. Bd3! Bf3

Same-Color Bishops: Drawing and Winning Methods

Diagram 284
White to move
What's his winning *plan*?

THE TWO MAIN METHODS OF DEFENSE IN THIS KIND OF ENDING ARE:

- Creation by the weaker side of a "fortress" of pawns and pieces, which blocks the opponent's king from advancing.
- The rule of the one diagonal. It is important that the bishop act on one diagonal while preventing the movements of the opponent's king and pawns. Defending on two diagonals could be dangerous because the opponent may create zugzwang or distract or decoy on one diagonal and break through on the other.

TO WIN, THE SUPERIOR SIDE DEPENDS ON:

- Effective support by his king for his passed pawn.
- Or the advance of an outside passed pawn to decoy the defender's forces so that the superior side's king can decisively penetrate and assault his opponent's now defenseless pawns.

Solution: White wins by using his outside passed pawn to distract the enemy king, guarding his own pawns with his bishop, and attacking and capturing the enemy pawns with his king. Therefore, he will play Bc3 and Be1, and move his king via the light squares to f7.

Diagram 285

5. Ke3, draw.

Also good is 5. Bc2.

OTHER STRATEGIES

The main factor in bishop endings is the position of the pawns, which in turn determines which bishops are good and bad. But there are other elements of strategy—such as remote passed pawns and the position of the kings—significant in endings with the same color bishops.

Let's look at the following study, created by the second World Chess Champion.

EM. LASKER

Diagram 286
White to move

White first bolsters the position of his king as much as possible.

1. Bc3 Bd6 2. Ke3 Kf7 3. Ke4 Ke6

Now White advances his distant, passed pawn to divert Black's pieces from the center.

4. b4 Bc7 5. b5 Kf6

Diagram 287

6. g4!

White further strengthens his position. Worse is 6. Kd5 because of 6. ... Kf5 7. Kc6 Bd8.

6. ... Ke6 7. g5

Makes f6 off-limits for the opposing king. This fact is here more important than the disadvantage of the pawn being on the same color square as White's bishop.

7. ... g6 8. Bb2

Black is in zugzwang.

**8. ... Bd6 9. b6 Bb8 10. b7 Bd6 11. Ba3 Bc7
12. Bb4 Kd7**

Or 12. ... Bb8 13. Bc5, still forcing Black's king to move.

Diagram 288

13. Kd5 Bb8 14. Bc5 e4 15. Be3 Kc7 16. Bf4+ Kxb7 17. Bxb8 Kxb8 18. Kxe4 Kc7 19. Ke5 Kd7 20. Kf6, winning.

Part 2: Bishops of Opposite Color

The most drawish of all endings are those with lone bishops traveling on opposite-color squares. The great chance of a draw in these bishops-of-opposite-color ("BOC," for short) endings is a result of the weaker side's having, in effect, an extra piece for defense. Not just one extra pawn, but two (or even three) are often not enough to win. So the stronger side should enter these endings warily, while the weaker side should welcome them.

Even great players err in these tricky endings. Pawn sacrifices, some quite surprising, are more common in these endgames than in any other, even rook-and-pawn endings, since the remaining pawns may not be dangerous. Capablanca's admonition to avoid thinking only in concrete terms, and to think also in terms of themes applies especially to bishops-of-opposite-color endgames. And Capa's famous rule of good and bad bishops is excellent advice to recall here as well: if your opponent has a bishop, place your pawns on the same color as his bishop; if you have a bishop, place the pawns on the opposite color of your bishop, regardless of whether your opponent has a bishop and what color it travels on.

GOOD FORTRESSES REQUIRE BAD BISHOPS!

Capa's exhortation to have a good bishop is particularly applicable to the stronger side in a BOC ending, especially when he has connected, passed pawns. As with any "rule," there are exceptions to this one. BOC endings provide a big exception. You'll see that in many of these endings you can cement a defensive *fortress* by putting your pawns on the same color squares as your bishop.

In fact the weaker side often draws because he can rely on a "bad" bishop and his "wrong"-color pawns! He constructs one of two kinds of fortresses—the king fortress and the bishop fortress. Here's an example of a *king's fortress*.

An impregnable *king's fortress*—the defending king stops the passed pawn, while his bishop guards his own pawn on the other side of the board and prevents the creation of new passers.

Diagram 289
Example of a *king's fortress*
No matter who is to move, Black holds easily.
(Note that if Black's h-pawn were on h7, White to move
wins with 1. h6 and 2. Be4, creating a second passed pawn.)

In a king's fortress, the defender's king blocks the pawn. In a bishop's fortress, the bishop blocks the pawn. The king's fortress is usually easier to hold.

PASSED PAWNS

As usual, connected passed pawns are very strong, but only if unblocked. If the pawns are isolated, the greater the number of files between them, the greater the winning chances.

Diagram 290

Another typical example of a fortress created by Black. Despite the large material advantage, White can't advance his passed pawns and can't create any new passed pawns. Black's king and bishop block the passed pawns. He can simply shuffle his bishop back and forth to draw. Become comfortable with this technique. It can be your frequent path to a draw in BOC endings!

Black's task is more complicated in the following position.

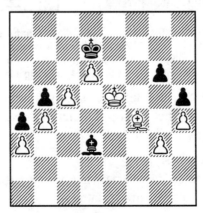

Diagram 291
White to move

White can try to get to e6 or e7 by sacrificing the c-pawn. This plan does not work immediately: 1. c6+ Kxc6 2. Ke6 Bf5+ 3. Ke7 Bg4, and Black controls d7. But White can try to take the f5-base from Black's bishop.

1. g4

If 1. ... hxg4?, then 2. h5 gxh5 3. c6+ Kxc6 4. Ke6.

Diagram 292
After 4. Ke6

Now Black has to give up his bishop for the d-pawn and lose— for example, 4. ... h4 5. d7 Bf5+ 6. Kxf5 Kxd7 7. Kxg4 Ke6 8. Kxh4 Kd5 9. Kg5 Kc4 10. Kf5 Kb3 11. Ke4 Kxa3 12. Bd6 Kb3 13. Kd4 a3 14. Kc5 a2 15. Be5 +-.

But, in Diagram 292, Black has a saving move.

1. ... Be2

This knocks White's plans into a cocked hat.

2. gxh5

Or 2. g5 Bg4 3. Kf6 Bf5 =.

2. ... gxxh5 3. c6+ Kxc6 4. Ke6 Bg4+.

The great drawing potential of the opposite-color bishops is well illustrated by the following position, an example of the second kind of fortress, the bishop's fortress.

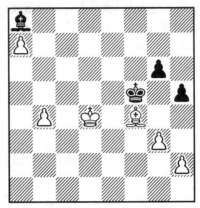

Diagram 293
White to move

White can't win because his opponent's king and bishop block his king and pawns—for example,

1. Kc5 Ke6 2. Kb6 Kd7 3. b5 Kc8! draw.

Not 3. ... Bf3? because of 4. a8(Q)! Bxa8 5. Ka7 Bf3 6. Kb8! Be4 7. b6 Kc6 8. Ka7, winning.

> A bishop's fortress—the bishop stops the passed pawn while the king protects his own pawns and tries to prevent the creation of new ones. As the diagram at right shows, with a bishop's fortress, the defender must stay especially alert.

Diagram 294
After 6. Kb8!

The winning plan in such positions is usually to bring the king to support the passed pawn to win bishop for pawn. The defending bishop can't hold by itself; it requires coordination with its king. Therefore, given a choice, the defender should try to block the passer with his own king, preferring a king's fortress.

DON'T OVERBURDEN YOUR BISHOP

Just as in same-color-bishop endings, it's always better when your bishop can do its work on one diagonal. In the following position, the bishop's role in stopping White's two passed pawns on the same diagonal (b8-h2) is particularly visible.

Diagram 295
White to move

Black's bishop is ideally placed, and White can't make any progress.

1. Kd5 Kf6 2. Kc5 Ke7 3. Kb5 Bf4 4. Kb6 Kd8, draw.

Take a new look at Diagram 295 and imagine the pawn not on f3 but on g4. The defense would then fail.

Diagram 296
White wins

IT'S NOT *ALWAYS* A DRAW!

For a change of pace, let's look at a couple of endings where the stronger side can actually manage to win!

KOTOV—BOTVINNIK
MOSCOW, 1955

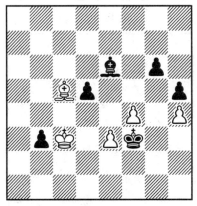

Diagram 297
White to move

On first impression, the position is drawn: White's king covers the pawn on b3, and his own pawns are well protected by his bishop (another case where the "bad" bishop is a good defensive tool). But Black has a pleasing way to infiltrate with his king, allowing him to create a second passed pawn.

1. ... g5! 2. fxg5.

If 2. hxg5, then 2. ... h4 3. Bd6 Bf5! (see diagram) 4. g6 Bxg6 5. Kxb3 Kg2 6. Kc3 h3 7. f5 Bxf5 8. Kd4 Be4 -+.

Diagram 298
After 3. ... Bf5!

Fortress Building
& Maintenance 101

Remember, even though you can be one, two, or three pawns down in bishops-of-opposite-color endings, you may still draw.

Quality of the pawns is more important than quantity! Think creatively. Drawing in bishops-of-opposite-color endings when you're material down is most often accomplished by building a fortress. Here's the short course.

Diagram 299
White to move
This position by Mark Dvoretsky illustrates in a nutshell most of the key principles of fortress building.

- ♚ Think *theme*, not *moves*! Build, don't just play.
- ♚ A fortress, once built, requires little defense. The weaker side shuffles back and forth, staying "inside" the barricade he's created.
- ♚ Target enemy pawns, forcing them to move to a wrong-color square or be defended.
- ♚ The stronger side should advance connected passers by leading with the pawn that goes to a square the same color covered by his opponent's bishop. When he doesn't, the defender has the beginnings of a fortress. (See solution below.)
- ♚ Nuance is often more important than material.
- ♚ Both sides should respect the principle of "the same diagonal."

Diagram 300

THE STRONGER SIDE SHOULD ADVANCE HIS CONNECTED PAWNS TO SQUARES OF THE COLOR *NOT* COVERED BY HIS OWN BISHOP.

SOLUTION
1. c5! (clearing the diagonal!) 1. ... Bxc5
2. Bb3 (targeting the e-pawn, forcing it to the wrong color square, allows the perfect blockade) 2. ... e5 3. Be6 Kc7 4. Ke4 (see diagram above).

White has built his fortress. He now simply moves his bishop from f5 to g4 and back.

For the defender, a passed pawn is usually less useful than a defensive pawn.

If, in the diagram at top, it's Black's move, he should win. Note that if you move the c-pawn to the kingside or to d3, it's a draw, no matter who moves.

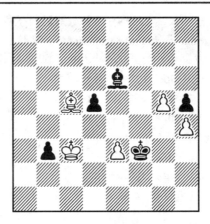

Diagram 301

2. ... d4+!

Black must preserve his b3-pawn to maintain a distant distraction, "spreading" the defense. Black is down a pawn, but his passed pawns decide the outcome of the game.

3. exd4

Or 3. Bxd4 Kg3 4. g6 Kxh4 5. Kd2 Kh3!

Diagram 302
After 5. ... Kh3!

6. Bf6 h4 7. Ke2 Kg2 -+.

FOR THE DEFENDER, A PASSED PAWN IS USUALLY LESS VALUABLE THAN A PAWN WELL PLACED TO *DEFEND*.

Diagram 303

3. ... Kg3

Precise until the end! After the careless 3. ... Kg4?, White saves himself with 4. d5! Bxd5 5. Bf2.

4. Ba3 Kxh4 5. Kd3 Kxg5 6. Ke4 h4 7. Kf3 Bd5+

Diagram 304

White resigns. Black's king will go to c2, forcing his opponent to give up a bishop for a pawn. Note that Black's bishop will protect his h-pawn and stop White's d-pawn on the same h3-c8 diagonal.

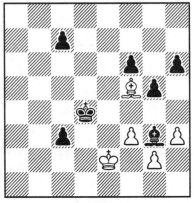

Diagram 305
White to move

Black can't win without creating a passed pawn on the king-side. It is a good learning experience to study carefully the winning plan. It consists of three steps:

- ♚ the transfer of the king to g3;
- ♚ the advance of the kingside pawns;
- ♚ the creation of a passed pawn by means of a breakthrough.

1. ... Ke5 2. Bc2 Kf4 3. Bb1 Bh2 4. Kf2 Bg1+!

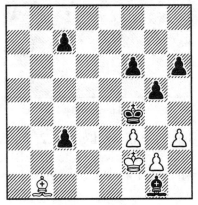

Diagram 306

5. Ke2

If 5. Kxg1 Ke3 6. Kf1 Kd2 -+.

5. ... Kg3 6. Kf1 Bf2 7. Bc2 f5! 8. Bb1

If 8. Bxf5, then 8. ... Kf4, winning a decisive tempo for his king, which advances with 9. ... Ke3 and later ... Kd2.

8. ... f4 9. Bg6 Be3 10. Bc2 h5 11. Bf5 c5 12. Bg6 h4 13. Bf5 g4

Diagram 307

14. hxg4

No better is 14. fxg4 f3 15. gxf3 Kxh3.

14. ... h3 15. gxh3 Kxf3 16. g5 Kg3 17. g6 Bd4 18. h4 f3 19. h5 Bg7

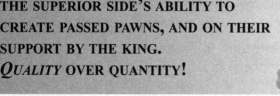

SUCCESS IN ENDINGS WITH DIFFERENT-COLOR BISHOPS DEPENDS LESS ON MATERIAL ADVANTAGE AND MORE ON THE SUPERIOR SIDE'S ABILITY TO CREATE PASSED PAWNS, AND ON THEIR SUPPORT BY THE KING.
QUALITY OVER QUANTITY!

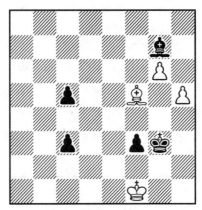

Diagram 308

20. Ke1 f2+ 21. Kf1 Kf3, White resigns.

CONNECTED PASSED PAWNS—
THE THREE RULES OF DEFENSE

Practice applying the principles for drawing in bishop-of-opposite-color endgames by analyzing the positions below, in which bishop and pawns are opposed by a lone bishop. You'll understand these endings more deeply in just a few well directed moments!

In positions where king, bishop and two connected passed pawns (that are well placed, but not far advanced) oppose king and lone bishop, the defense can hold. But conditions must be just right:

> ♗The defending bishop must restrain the "right" pawn from advancing, ready to sacrifice itself for both pawns, drawing.

> ♗Attack the opponent's pawn, thus preventing the enemy king from maneuvering.

> ♗At the same time, the bishop must always have a spare square on the diagonal in order to avoid zugzwang.

TARRASCH

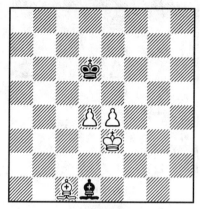

Diagram 309
White to move

If White can advance his connected, passed pawns to the sixth
rank, he will win. Black should try to prevent this plan.

1. Ba3+

If 1. d5, then 1. ... Bh5 and 2. ... Bf7, with the same plan as
before.

1. ... Kd7 2. d5 Bh5!

2. ... Bb3 loses because of 3. Kd4 Bc2 4. e5 (see diagram) 4. ...
Ba4 (this equals resignation, but 4. ... Bf5 5. Ke3 Bg4 6. Kf4
also wins for White; see also Diagram 313) 5. e6+ Ke8 6. d6
Bc6 7. Bc1 Ba4 8. Bg5 Bc6 9. Kc5 Ba4 10. Kb6 +-.

Diagram 310
After 4. e5

Diagram 311

3. e5

If 3. Kf4, then 3. ... Bg6! 4. Bf4 Bh7 (targeting).

3. ... Bf7! 4. Kd4 Bg8!

Diagram 312

A key position! This important defensive formation is constructed according to the three rules given on page 240—along with the precept that the weaker side's bishop should attack his opponent's pawns from the *front*. The position is drawn because White can't move his king away from the d5-pawn.

Put the Black bishop on g4 (as in Diagram 313), and the White king would be free to move, in violation of defensive rule number two. White wins by going to f6 to support his pawn's advance to e6.

Diagram 313

BERGER

Diagram 314
White to move

1. Bf3 Kd8 2. Ke6 Bb4 3. f6 Ba3 4. f7

WITH NO OTHER PAWNS ON THE BOARD, TWO
ISOLATED PAWNS, SEPARATED BY ONLY ONE
FILE, USUALLY DO NOT WIN. BUT WHEN
THE PAWNS ARE SEPARATED BY *TWO*
FILES OR MORE, THEY OFTEN WIN.
THE FURTHER THEY'RE SEPARATED,
THE BETTER THE WINNING CHANCES.

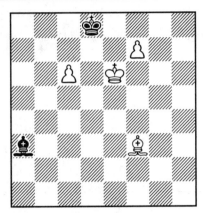

Diagram 315

4. ... Bb4 5. Kf6 Bc3+ 6. Kg6 Bb4 7. Kg7, winning.

TARGETING

The following position is important to understand for two reasons—it shows how to fight against separated pawns and, even more importantly, it illustrates the effectiveness of targeting.

BERGER—KOTLERMAN
MINSK, 1949

Diagram 316
White to move and draw—
if he's taken "Fortress Building 101"

White's defense is clever. He gives his opponent the opportunity to advance his b-pawn. But if Black does push his pawn, he blocks his own king. White also gives Black the opportunity to move his king ahead of his pawn. But if Black does this, he limits his own king's movement.

1. Bg6 Kb2

Or 1. ... b2 2. Bb1, creating an impregnable fortress.

2. Bf7!

Targeting! This move ties the king to the defense of the pawn and, most importantly, thus prevents Black's from playing ... Ka1, followed by ... b2, winning.

2. ... Ka2

If 2. ... Kc3, then 3. Be6 is the simplest—for example, 3. ... b2 4. Bf5 Kb3 5. Bb1 or 3. ... Kd3 4. Bf5+ Kc3 5. Be6, with a draw.

3. Be6 Ka3 4. Bf5, draw.

TARGETING—ATTACKING A PAWN IN ORDER TO PROVOKE IT TO MOVE TO A WRONG-COLORED SQUARE OR TO TIE THE ENEMY KING TO ITS DEFENSE—IS A COMMON AND VERY EFFECTIVE TECHNIQUE IN FORTRESS BUILDING AND MAINTENANCE.

Summary: *Your bishops are a unique duo in your army because they can never support each other, nor can they cover the same square.*

Same-color bishop endings are not particularly drawish because the opposing bishops can make head-to-head contact. When one opponent is a single pawn up, the defending side looks for a chance to sacrifice his bishop for the pawn, drawing instantly. The outcome of the fight often depends on whether his bishop, after being forced to the short diagonal covering the pawn, always has a waiting move, so that his king isn't forced to give way. Bishop and two pawns against bishop is usually a win, but there are some drawish positions, especially on the edge of the board.

When both sides have pawns, their locations are critical. Having or creating a passed pawn is once again the key to victory. To win, you must have effective king support for your passed pawn, or an outside passed pawn to decoy defenders so that you can penetrate with your king to capture the enemy pawns on the other side of the board.

A "bad" bishop can lead to a loss, while with a good bishop a defender can often draw a pawn down.

Bishops-of-opposite-color endings are the most drawish type of endgame. Frequently the fortress technique leads to a draw, even when the defender is more than a single pawn down. Through the technique of targeting the enemy pawns—attacking them to force them to either be defended, thus tying down the opposing king, or forced to a wrong-color square—the defender can help to build his fortress. There are two types of fortresses.

In the king's fortress, the defender's king blocks the passed pawn and his bishop guards his own pawns on the other side of the board. At the same time, the defender's pieces guard against the creation of new passed pawns. The king's fortress is the easiest to maintain—once built, the defender just shuffles his pieces to draw.

In the bishop's fortress, the roles of the defender's pieces are reversed. His bishop blocks the passed pawn and his king guards his own pawns on the other side of the board. This kind of fortress is much trickier to maintain, because the attacker can try to move his king to support his passed pawn, push it and force the defending bishop to sacrifice itself for it. Therefore, the bishop's fortress requires careful coordination between the defender's king and bishop.

For defenders, a passed pawn is usually not as valuable as a well placed defensive pawn. Quality of the pawns is much more important than their quantity. The ability of one side to create passed pawns is crucial to the outcome of the game.

As always in any kind of bishop endgame, it's better if your bishop can do all of its work on one diagonal.

Bishop Endings
Learning Exercises

Diagram 317
White to move

Diagram 318
White to move

Diagram 319
Black to move

Diagram 320
White to move

Diagram 321
White to move

Diagram 322
White to move

Bishop Endings
Solutions

Diagram 323
White to move

Diagram 324
Black to move

No. 1   **1. Bg7 Bc1 2. Bh6 Bb2** (2. ... Ba3 3. Bg5 Bf8 4. Bf6 Kf4
5. Bg7 +-) **3. Bg5 Bg7 4. Be7 Bb2 5. h6, followed by
6. Bf8 and 7. Bg7.**

No. 2   **1. Ba6! Kc6** (1. ... b6 2. Bxc8= ; 1. ... bxa6=) **2. Bxb7+! =.**

No. 3   **1. ... Bh4! 2. gxh4** (or 2. Bd4 Bxg3-+) **2. ... g3 3. hxg3 h2 -+.**

No. 4   **1. b4!** (1. Bd5 h3 2. Bc4 h2 3. Bd5 Be6 4. Bf3 Bxb3 5. Kg3 Bd1!
6. Kxh2 Bxf3 7. Kg3 Be4 8. Kf4 Bf5 9. Ke3 Ke5 -+,
since White's king can't reach the a1-square) **1. ... axb4 2. a5 Ke7
3. a6 Kd6 4. a7 Bb7 5. Kg4 =.**

No. 5   **1. Bf2+ Kh5 2. g4+ Kh6 3. Kf6 Kh7 4. g5 Kh8 5. Bd4 Kh7
6. Ba1 Kh8 7. g6 fxg6 8. Kxg6 mate.**

No. 6   **1. Ba6 Ke4** (1. ... Bf6 2. Bc4 Ke5 3. Kd3=) **2. Bc4 Bf6
3. Ba6 Kd5 4. Kd3 Kc6** (4. ... e2 5. Bc4+!) **5. Kc2! Kb6
6. Be2 Ka5 7. Kb3 Be7 8. Bf1 =.**

No. 7   **1. e6 fxe6 2. fxe6 Bxe6 3. Ke5 Bb3 4. Kd6 c4 5. Kc5 Kf5
6. Kb4 a2 7. Ka3 Ke4 8. Kb2 Kd3 9. Ka1 =.**

No. 8   **1. ... Bc2 2. Bd6** (2. c4 b6-+) **a3! 3. bxa3 Kxc3 and after
... Ba4, and ... b5 Black's king marches to g2.**

Chapter 7: Knight Against Bishop
Some Important Ideas to Look For

◆ The knight blocks the Black bishop to shelter the pawn's march to promotion.

White has just played 14. Nd6.

See Diagram 330.

◆ White is in zugzwang—he moves and loses.

Black has just played 10. ... Bf2.
See Diagram 344.

◆ Black's knight is corralled.

White plays 1. Bd4!.
See Diagram 353.

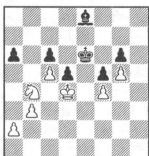

◆ Black's bad bishop can't compete with the knight.

White has just played 8. Nb4.
See Diagram 364.

Chapter 7
Knight against Bishop:

White (and Black) Bishops Can't Jump!

Apologies to the popular basketball movie, but our chapter subtitle helps us make an important point. It's often said that the knight and the bishop are about equal. But, although these two "players" may be of roughly the same overall importance to the team, their talents are very different. They're equal only in the same sense that a star basketball center is equal to a league-leading guard, or that an all-star baseball pitcher is the equivalent of the team's homerun king. Your at-the-moment preference depends on the situation you're in.

PLAY WITH ONE PAWN ON THE BOARD

The short-hopping knight covers distances slowly, but has the unique ability to vault other pieces. It can reach every square on the board. The fast-moving bishop can cross the entire board in a single move—if its path is clear. But it's limited to only the squares of its own color. Thus it can never lay a miter on one-half of the playing field. The striking difference between these two "minor pieces," as we sometimes call them, can be illustrated by analyzing play with a single pawn on the board.

KOSHEK

Diagram 325
White to move

White can win only if his knight can block the bishop from capturing the advancing pawn.

1. Nd6 Bg1 2. c6 Bb6 3. Ke6

Diagram 326

In order to play 4. Kd7 Kg2 5. Nc4, pushing the bishop from the a5-d8 diagonal.

3. ... Bc7 4. Kd7 Bb8 5. Nb5 Kg2 6. Nc7 Kf3
7. Kc8 Ba7 8. Nb5

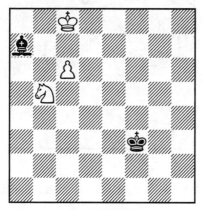

Diagram 327

8. ... Bb6

If 8. ...Be3, then 9. Nd6 Bb6 10. Kd7 and 11. Nc4+-.

9. Kb7 Bd8

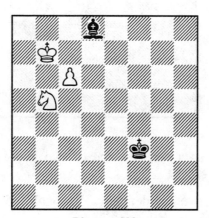

Diagram 328

After 9. ... Ba5 10. Nd6 Bd8, Black would be lost because of 11. Kc8 Ba5 12. Kd7 and 13. Nc4, or 10. ... Kf4 11. Nc4 Bd8 12. Kc8 Bh4 13. Kd7+-.

10. Nd6 Kg4 11. Kc8 Ba5 12. Nc4

Diagram 329

12. ... Be1 13. Kd7 Bg3 14. Nd6, winning.

Diagram 330

Black's loss was a consequence of two key elements of the position:

- One of the two key defensive diagonals (a5-d8) was too short—only four squares;

- His king was far removed from the action. ·

❖ ❖ ♚ ❖ ❖

WITH THE ENEMY KING OUT OF ACTION, A KNIGHT AND PAWN CAN BLOCK THE BISHOP FROM CAPTURING AN ADVANCING PASSED PAWN ONLY IF THE SHORTER DIAGONAL IS MADE UP OF FOUR SQUARES OR LESS.

With five squares on a short diagonal it is impossible to block a bishop. Let's take a look.

AVERBAKH

Diagram 331
White to move

1. Ke6 Bb5 2. Ke7 Bc6 3. Kd8 Bb5 4. Kc7 Kg1

With a defensive diagonal of five squares or more for the defending bishop, there's no need for the king to leave his corner.

5. Nd3 Kh1 6. Ne5

With the threat of 7. Nc6.

Diagram 332

6. ... Be8 7. Nd7 Kg1 8. Kd8 Bg6 9. Ke7 Bf5 10. Nc5

Diagram 333

10. ... Bc8

Parrying the immediate threat of 11. Ne6.

11. Nd7 Kh1 12. Kd8 Ba6 13. Kc7 Bb5 14. Ne5 Be8!, draw.

Diagram 334

When bishop and pawn oppose the knight, the stronger side's main objective is to push the knight away from the path of the passed pawn. This goal is often achieved by zugzwang.

Unlike the bishop, which by itself may successfully defend against the passed pawn (supported by king and knight), the knight cannot alone stop the pawn.

BRON

Diagram 335
White to move

White should first push Black's king back, while preventing the knight from checking.

1. Bb3 Kf5 2. Bf7 Kg5

If 2. ... Ke5, then 3. Be6 (Black's in zugzwang) 3. ... Ne4 4. d7+-.

3. Be6 Kg6 4. Kf8!

Diagram 336

4. ... Nh7+

If 4. ... Kg5, then 5. Kf7 +-, because Black is again in zugzwang. Or 4. ... Kh6 5. Kf7 Kg5 6. Bh3, and it's another zugzwang and a win for White.

5. Ke8

"Passing" a tempo by triangulation.

5. ... Nf6+ 6. Ke7 Kg7 7. Bf7

Zugzwang again!

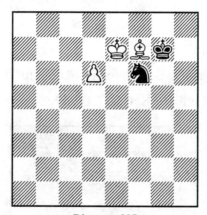

Diagram 337

7. ... Ng4 8. Bd5

Not 8. d7? Ne5 9. d8(Q) Nc6+ =.

> *In the ending, we must convert into a win any advantages*
> *won during the opening or middlegame.*
> *—Paul Keres*

Diagram 338

8. ... Ne5

If 8. ... Nf6, then 9. Be4 Ng8+ 10. Ke6 Nf6 11. Bf5, winning.

9. Be4 Kg8 10. Ke6 Nf7 11. d7

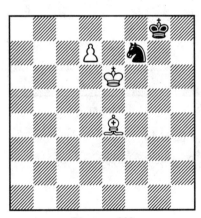

Diagram 339

11. ... Kf8

If 11. ... Nd8+ 12. Ke7, or 11. ... Kg7 12. Ke7 Kg8 13. Bd5.

12. Bd5, winning.

Note that White controls all squares available for the knight after 12. ... Nd8+ 13. Kd6 Kg7 14. Ke7.

Diagram 340
Black to move

Here, Black has an opportunity to sacrifice his knight so that his king can reach the h8 square, obtaining a position that's a well known draw—1. ... Nd3 2. h4 Nf4 3. Kf5 Kd6!. Instead, Black made a fatal mistake.

1. ... Ke4? 2. Bc8! Kf4

On 2. ... Nd3, White has 3. Bf5+, winning.

3. h4 Nf3 4. h5 Ng5 5. Bf5

Diagram 341

5. ... Nf3 6. h6 Ng5 7. Kg6, winning.

Black was forced into a zugzwang and lost, because White's pawn can't be stopped.

PLAY WITH MULTIPLE PAWNS

In Diagram 342, the battle ranges across the entire board, and the advantage of the bishop over the knight is obvious. The knight cannot quickly move from one side of the board to another. Additionally, it is tied down to the defense of the pawn. White is nearly in zugzwang. His knight is defending a pawn, and his king must stay at e2 so that he can respond f2-f3 to the threat of ... f5-f4-f3. He's left with only pawn moves, and none are satisfactory. He could try 1. b3 Be7 2. a4 f4, but would still have the same difficulties he faces in the game.

KOENIG—SMYSLOV
ENGLAND — USSR MATCH, 1946

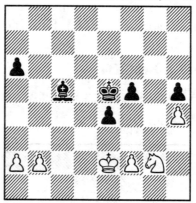

Diagram 342
White to move

1. a3 Bd6 2. b4 f4 3. f3 Kd4

Now that his king controls the d3-square, Black intends to further pin down his opponent's forces with e4-e3. So White must trade this pawn off.

4. fxe4 Kxe4 5. Ne1 Kd4

Diagram 343

White is defenseless against the Black king's penetration—6.
Kd2 Kc4 7. Kc2 Bb8 8. Nf3 Ba7 9. Ng5 Bb6 10. Nf3 Bf2.

Diagram 344
After 10. ... Bf2

Zugzwang. That's why White elects desperate counterplay in
the center. From the position in Diagram 343, White plays …

6. Kf3

**IN BISHOP VS. KNIGHT ENDINGS, THE
SIDE WITH THE KNIGHT IS A POTENTIAL
VICTIM OF ZUGZWANG. A KNIGHT,
UNLIKE A BISHOP, CANNOT MOVE
WHILE CONTINUING TO GUARD
THE SAME SQUARE.**

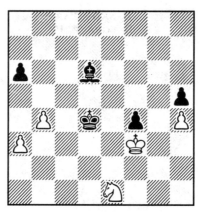

Diagram 345

6. ... Kc4 7. Ke4 Kb3 8. Nd3 Kxa3 9. Nc5 Kxb4, White resigns.

Diagram 346

After 10. Nxa6+ Kb5, the knight is corralled for keeps.

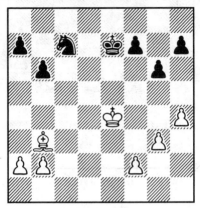

BENKO—PARMA
BELGRADE, 1964

Diagram 347
White to move

Black does not have any visible weaknesses. But the domination of the White bishop over his counterpart, along with the threat of penetration by the White king, ties down Black's forces. White starts the pawn attack on the kingside, trying to create a path for penetration.

1. f4 h6 2. Bc4 Kf6

No knight moves are good. For example 2. ... Ne6 3. Kd5 Kd7 4. Bb5+, and the White king penetrates on one side or the other.

3. g4 Ke7 4. Ke5 f6+ 5. Ke4 Kf8 6. h5

IN POSITIONS WITH SEVERAL PAWNS, THE COMPARATIVE ADVANTAGE OF A BISHOP (OR KNIGHT) DEPENDS ON THE PAWN STRUCTURE. THE BISHOP IS USUALLY STRONGER IN THE OPEN POSITIONS, ESPECIALLY WITH PLAY ON BOTH SIDES AND IN THE PRESENCE OF PASSED PAWNS.

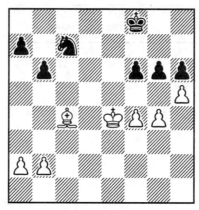

Diagram 348

6. ... g5

If 6. ... f5+, then 7. Ke5 fxg4 8. hxg6 g3 9. Bf1 Kg7 10. f5 h5 11. Kf4 h4 12. Kg5 Nd5 13. Bh3!.

Diagram 349
After 13. Bh3!

And White, as GM Pal Benko demonstrated, is winning.

7. fxg5 fxg5 8. Kf5 Kg7 9. Ke5

The attack by the White pawns has disorganized Black's position.

Diagram 350

Black doesn't have a satisfactory defense to the threatened penetration by the White king.

> **9. ... Ne8 10. Be6 Nf6 11. b4 Ne8 12. b5 Nf6 13. a4 Ne8 14. Bf5 Nf6 15. Ke6 Ne8 16. Be4 Nf6 17. Bf3 Ng8 18. Kd6**

Diagram 351

Preparation is done. White's king advances on the queenside pawns. White's pawns are all on the "wrong" squares, but he's winning! It's important to be specific and concrete in your analysis!

> **18. ... Kf8 19. Kc6 Ke7 20. Kb7 Kd6 21. Kxa7 Kc5 22. Ka6 Nf6 23. Bc6**

Zugzwang.

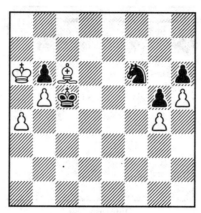

Diagram 352

**23. ... Nxg4 24. a5 bxa5 25. b6 Ne5 26. Be8,
Black resigns.**

**BELAVENETS—ILJIN-GENEVSKY
TBILISI, 1937**

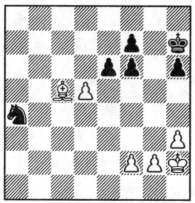

Diagram 353
White to move

This is another position that illustrates a fundamental idea.
After 1. dxe6 fxe6 (1. ...Nxc5? 2. e7 +-), the game is a draw, but
White found an interesting possibility of playing for a win.

1. Bd4!

An important technique to know in endings with bishop against the knight. Now the knight doesn't have a single move!

1. ... Kg7

A forced move. If 1. ... e5, Black loses to 2. d6. And after 1. ... exd5 2. Kg3 Kg6 3. Kf4, Black is in zugzwang and loses all of his pawns!

2. d6 Kf8 3. Bxf6

As a result, White has an extra pawn. The approach of the king finishes the game.

3. ... Nb6 4. Kg3 Nd7 5. Bb2 Kg8 6. Kg4 Kh7 7. Kh5 Nf8 8. g4 Nd7 9. g5

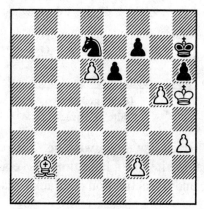

Diagram 354

9. ... hxg5 10. Kxg5 Kg8 11. Bd4 Kh7 12. h4 Nf8?

Losing right away. Better was to hold on with ... Kg8 and ... Kh7. Then in order to win, White would put his pawn on h6, station his bishop on g7, and move his king to the queenside.

13. Kf6, Black resigns.

THE KNIGHT CAN BE THE "SPRINGER OF SURPRISES"!

Here's one more piece of practical advice for playing with a bishop against knight, and from an unimpeachable expert. Tigran Petrosian, the ninth World Champion, called the knight the most subtle chess piece. It produces the unexpected in a way that the bishop cannot. So be careful! When playing against this surprise-artist, you must be accurate until the end.

Let's look at an example of what Petrosian was talking about.

Diagram 355
White to move

At first glance, Black has the advantage. The position is open, and it seems that White has a hard time preventing penetration by Black's king and the activation of Black's bishop. But White has a surprise.

1. c6! bxc6 2. Kb3

White threatens 3. a4 and 4. Nc4, mate.

2. ... Kb5

After 2. ... Bc5 White plays 3. Nc4+ Kb5 4. a4 mate. After other moves, Black loses his bishop to a fork.

3. a4+ Kc5 4. Nd7+

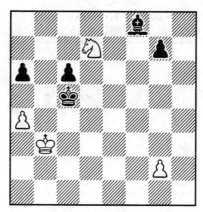

Diagram 356

4. ... Kd4 5. Nxf8 Ke3 6. Ng6 Kf2 7. Kc4 Kxg2 8. Kc5, winning.

THE KNIGHT CAN BE STRONGER IN CLOSE QUARTERS AND CLOSED POSITIONS

The knight is often stronger than the bishop when the confrontation is confined to a limited part of the board. The knight also shows itself to advantage in closed positions with stable pawn chains and is particularly effective against the "bad" bishop that is blocked by its own pawns.

Chess is a matter of delicate judgment,
knowing when to punch and how to duck.
—Bobby Fischer

IVASHIN—KONSTANTINOV
USSR, 1946

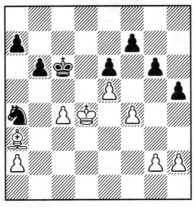

Diagram 357
Black to move

The organic weakness of White's position is the location of his own pawns on e5 and f4—squares the same color as his bishop. Black is planning to get to those pawns. First, he has to push White's king away.

1. ... b5 2. cxb5+ Kxb5 3. h3 a6 4. g4

White's last move is dubious because it weakens the f4-pawn. In any case, it would have been difficult for White to prevent Black's penetration of the light squares.

4. ... hxg4 5. hxg4 Nb6 6. Bd6 a5 7. Bf8 a4

Diagram 358

8. a3

In order to prevent 8. ... Nd5 and 9. ... Nb4.

8. ... Kc6

Trying immediately to move the knight to c6 doesn't work. For example: 8. ... Nd7 9. Bd6, or 8. ... Nc8 9. Bc5. The king's move puts White in zugzwang. Now 9. Ke4 is bad because of 9. ... Nd5 10. Bd6 Kb5 and Kc4. Also bad is 9. Kc3 Nd5+ (highlighting the weakening of the f-pawn on move 4) 10. Kc4 Nxf4 11. Kb4 Nd3+ 12. Kxa4 Nxe5.

9. Bb4 Nd5 10. Bd2 Kb5 11. f5 gxf5 12. gxf5 Ne7

Diagram 359

The exchanges do not relieve the pressure on White's position, because he's left with weak pawns remaining on a3 and e5.

13. fxe6 fxe6 14. Bc3 Nc6+ 15. Ke4 Kc4 16. Bd2 Nd8!

The knight is going to c5 in order to push White's king back even further. It's not sufficient for Black to play 16. ... Kb3? 17. Bc1 Kc2 18. Bh6 Kb2 19. Bf8.

17. Bb4 Nb7 18. Bf8 Nc5+

Diagram 360

19. Ke3

The pawn ending is lost for White.

19. ... Kd5 20. Kd2 Nd7 21. Bg7

Diagram 361

The capture 21. ... Nxe5 22. Kc3 would give White some counter-chances, allowing him to activate his king. Black goes for the a-pawn.

21. ... Kc4 22. Kc2 Nb6 23. Kb2 Kd3 24. Ka2 Kc2 25. Bf6 Nc4 26. Bg7 Nd2 27. Bf8 Ne4 28. Bb4 Nc3+

Diagram 362

29. Ka1 Kb3 30. Bd6 Nb5, White resigns.

THE KNIGHT AGAINST THE BAD BISHOP

AVERBAKH—LILIENTHAL
MOSCOW, 1949

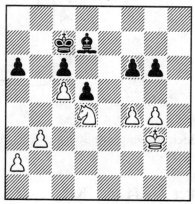

Diagram 363
White to move

Black has a "bad" bishop. White's plan is to penetrate on the dark squares.

1. g5! fxg5

If 1. ... f5, White plays 2. Nf3, and there could follow 2. ... Be8 3. Ne5 Kd8 4. Kf3 Ke7 5. Ke3 Ke6 6. Kd4 Ke7 7. Nd3 Ke6 8. Nb4

Diagram 364
After 8. Nb4

8. ... a5 9. Nd3 Bd7 10. a4 Be8 11. b4 axb4 12. Nxb4

Diagram 365
After 12. Nxb4

and 13. a5 +-. Back to Diagram 363.

2. fxg5 Bc8 3. Kf4 a5 4. Ke5

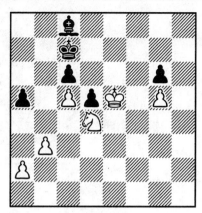

Diagram 366

4. ... Ba6

If 4. ... Bg4, then 5. Kf6 Bh5 6. Ne6+ Kd7 7. Nf4

Diagram 367
After 7. Nf4

Black loses one of his pawns. For example 7. ... Ke8 8. Ke6
Bf3 9. Kd6!

Diagram 368
After 9. Kd6!

9. ... Be4 (9. ... d4 10. Ke5) 10. Ne2 Bb1 11. a3 Bc2 12. Nd4. Back to the game (Diagram 366).

5. Kf6 Bd3

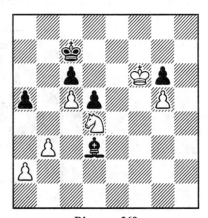

Diagram 369

White now pushes Black's king away and wins the pawn on c6.

6. Ke7 Bb1 7. a3 Be4 8. Ne6+ Kb7 9. Kd6 Bc2 10. Nd4 Bd1 11. Nxc6, winning.

In Diagram 370, the knight once again successfully blocks the passed pawn. The horseman is especially effective at this task when the pawn is on a square of the same color as its bishop.

**VAGANIAN—CHECHELIAN
RUSSIA, 1968**

**Diagram 370
Black to move**

With a pawn sacrifice, Black enables his king to infiltrate.

1. ... f4+! 2. Bxf4+ Kf5 3. Bd2

Or 3. Kf3 Nxd4+ 4. Ke3 Nc2+, followed by 5. ... Nxb4.

3. ... Ke4 4. Bc3 Kd3 5. Ba1 Kc2

**Diagram 371
Black to move**

This is more accurate than 5. ... Nxb4 6. Kf4 Nc6 7. Kf5.

6. Kf4 Kxb3 7. Kf5 Nxb4 8. Ke6 Kc4 9. Kd6 a5

Diagram 372

10. Bb2

10. c6 Nxc6! 11. Kxc6 a4 12. Kb6 a3 13. Ka5 a2 14. Kb6 b4
15. Ka5 Kb3, winning.

10. ... a4 11. Ba3 Na6 12. Kc6 b4 13. Kb6 Nb8!

Diagram 373
Black to move

14. Bc1 a3 15. Ka5

If 15. Kb7, Kxd4.

15. ... Nc6+, White resigns.

Summary: *We say that the bishop and knight are roughly equal, but the pieces are so different from one another that the specific characteristics of the ending really determine their comparative value. The success of a lone bishop defending against knight and pawn depends on how long the bishop's shortest diagonal is. Because bishops can zoom from one side of the board to the other, they're generally to be favored in open positions with pawns on both sides of the board. The knight is more vulnerable to zugzwang. But the "Springer of surprises" must always be watched carefully! The knight is more comfortable in endgames with all the pawns on one side of the board, and is better in close quarters, closed positions, and particularly excels against the "bad" bishop.*

Knight against Bishop
Learning Exercises

Diagram 374
Black to move

Diagram 375
White to move

Diagram 376
White to move

Diagram 377
Black to move

Diagram 378
White to move

Diagram 379
White to move

Knight against Bishop
Solutions

No. 1   **1. ... Bg5!** (1. ... Bd8 2. Ne5 Kh7 3. Ng4 Kh8 4. Nf6, zugzwang +-) **2. Ne5 Kh7 3. Ng4 Bd8 4. Nf6+ Kh6 =.**

No. 2   **1. Bg4 Kb5 2. Be2+ Kc5** (2. ... Ka5 3. Bc4) **3. Bc4 Nc6 4. b7 +-.**

No. 3   **1. g5 Ng8** (After 1. ... hxg5, either 2. h6 or 2. Bxf6, winning easily.) **2. gxf6 gxf6 3. Bc1 Kc7 4. Bd2 Kc6 5. Bf4 Kc7 6. e7!**

Diagram 380
After 6. e7!

6. ... Kd7 7. e8(Q)+ Kxe8 8. Kd5 Ne7+ 9. Ke6 +-.

No. 4   **1. ... Bb1 2. Nf1 Bc2 3. Nd2 Ke6 4. Kf2 d5 5. cxd5+ Kxd5 6. Ke3 Bd1**

Diagram 381
After 6. ... Bd1

(zugzwang) **7. Kd3 Bxb3! -+.**

No. 5   **1. b5 axb5 2. Bxb7 Nxb7 3. a6 Nd6 4. a7 and 5. a8(Q) +-.**

No. 6   **1. Kg8 Bg4** (1. ...Be4 2. Nxe6) **2. Ng6 Bd1 3. Nh8 Bh5 4. Kg7** (zugzwang) **+-.**

Chapter 8: Queen Endings
Some Important Ideas to Look For

◆Black can escape by finding a perpetual check.

Black plays 1. ... Qd1+.
See Diagram 385.

◆White's king and queen weave a mating net after 2. Kf3.

See Diagram 391.

◆White checks to escape with a draw.

See Diagram 397.

◆White has two plans: to push his pawn toward promotion, and to exchange queens in a way that leaves him with a winning pawn ending.

See Diagram 404.

Chapter 8
Queen Endings:

Ultimate Power on an Open Board

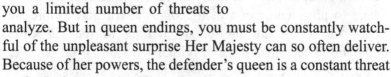

A queen in an endgame is like a rumor at a political convention—it travels so fast it seems to be everywhere at once. As we know, the queen is the most powerful piece in all stages of the game. As the ending approaches, the board empties of other pieces, lines open, and the queen radiates power in all directions. A pawn, a bishop— even a knight or rook—leaves you a limited number of threats to analyze. But in queen endings, you must be constantly watchful of the unpleasant surprise Her Majesty can so often deliver. Because of her powers, the defender's queen is a constant threat to check the opposite king relentlessly.

In the old days, we could count on a generalized "fifty-move" rule. If neither opponent had captured a man or moved a pawn in 50 moves, either player could claim a draw, regardless of the pieces and pawns on the board.

THE WEAKER SIDE SHOULD COUNT THE MOVES MADE AFTER THE LAST CAPTURE OR PAWN MOVE (WHICHEVER IS MOST RECENT) AND KEEP AN ACCURATE SCORE (NECESSARY FOR CLAIMING A DRAW OR A TIME FORFEIT). HE SHOULD KNOW THE UP-TO-DATE RULES AND CLAIM THE DRAW AS SOON AS IT'S LEGAL!

Then computers arrived. These tireless calculators have shown that there are positions—notably queen and pawn versus queen, and rook and bishop versus rook—that with best play require an extension of the 50-move rule to make progress! At first, the United States Chess Federation and FIDE (the World Chess Federation) changed their rules. But it then became apparent that these computer-discovered lines had little impact on human play. They're theoretically interesting but impractical in the hurly-burly world of tournament play.

So both organizations changed the rules back again! For example, in USCF play, unless the director publicizes the use of special endgame extensions, the general 50-move rule applies. The rules require that you keep an accurate scoresheet and that you make your claim to a director.

Perhaps computers, with their limitless attention span, and no desire to play tennis or watch *Jeopardy*, will have more surprises for us in the future. By writing to the US Chess Federation's technical director (USCF's address is on page 411 of this book), you can keep abreast of the latest rules.

Although the majority of GM games with queen and pawn versus queen (and the defending king far away) are won, these endgames are difficult for both sides. Some of the best defensive tips amount to the off-the-board techniques of knowing how to claim a draw!

QUEEN AND PAWN AGAINST QUEEN

Diagram 382   **Diagram 383**

Without kings, the pawn queens easily, no matter where the pawn is.

Let's look at some key, practical positions to learn the fundamental techniques in the battle of queen versus queen and pawn. First we'll look at a position that illustrates that when the weaker side's king helps to stop the pawn, the game is usually drawn—unless the stronger side has an immediate winning threat.

UNLESS THE DEFENDER CAN BLOCK THE PAWN WITH HIS KING, OR PERPETUALLY CHECK THE ENEMY KING, THE STRONGER SIDE WINS. INDEED, IF THERE WERE NO KINGS ON THE BOARD, THE STRONGER SIDE COULD ALWAYS FORCE HIS PAWN TO THE PROMOTION SQUARE. AS A RULE, THE FURTHER THE PAWN IS FROM THE CENTER, THE MORE DIFFICULT THE ENDING IS TO WIN.

Diagram 384

With White to move in this position, he plays 1. Qc4+, reducing the game to a simply won pawn ending—the king's in front of the pawn and has the direct opposition.

Black to move avoids this tactic and keeps the draw by 1. ... Qf1+ or, even simpler, by 1. ... Qd5.

Even on her own, the queen can often check the enemy king to a draw.

THE DEFENDER SHOULD BE ALERT TO THE THREE-TIME REPETITION OF ANY POSITION, AND IF IT OCCURS, CLAIM A DRAW. KEEP IN MIND THAT THE REPETITIONS DO *NOT* HAVE TO BE CONSECUTIVE! ONCE AGAIN, YOU'LL NEED AN ACCURATE SCORE.

Diagram 385
Black to move

1. ... Qd1+ 2. Kf2 Qd2+ 3. Kf3 Qd3+ 4. Kg4

Diagram 386

4. ... Qe2+!

Diagonal check—an important defensive tool in these endings.

After 4. ... Qg6+? 5. Kh4, White escapes the checks.

5. Kg5 Qg2+ 6. Kf5 Qc2+ 7. Ke6 Qc4+ 8. Kf5 Qc2+, draw.

There is no escape from the checks.

VELIMIROVIC—MARJANOVIC
BELGRADE, 1982

Diagram 387
White to move

Here the White king is protected by his own queen and pawn, so Black cannot achieve a perpetual check.

1. Ka7 Qa4+ 2. Kb6 Qb3+ 3. Ka5.

Remember this technique. The superior king moves toward the opponent's queen, paradoxically limiting her checking options.

3. ... Qa2+ 4. Kb5

Diagram 388

4. ... Qa8

Trying 4. ... Qb2+ would lead, after 5. Qb4+, to an easily won ending for White. The threat of queen exchanges is another important tool of the stronger side.

5. c7, White wins.

Now 5. ... Qb7+ loses to 6. Ka5 Qa8+ 7. Kb6 Qc8 8. Qc6!.

Diagram 389
After 8. Qc6!

White follows up with 9. Ka7 and 10. Qb7. If Black had tried 5. ... Qc8, White would win by the same technique: 6. Qd6+ Ke3 7. Kb6, as in the line above. In this example, the Black king's position on d2 provided White with additional opportunities to threaten a queen-exchanging check. The Black king would have been better posted on h2 or h3.

The strong side has three methods of avoiding pesky checks and pins:

- **Threaten to exchange queens by means of a counter-check;**
- **Move his king near his pawn to use it for shelter;**
- **Send his king into the lioness' den—move it closer to the opponent's queen to restrict her mobility.**

NEUMAN

Diagram 390
White to move

After the unexpected 1. Qd5!, Black makes a decisive mistake.

1. Qd5! Qxb4+?

Rejecting the Trojan-horse gift on b4 (for instance, with 1. ... Qg6+) would prolong resistance.

2. Kf3

This simple king move produces a fascinating position in which Black, despite having regained material balance, has no defense!

SOMETIMES IN QUEEN VS.
QUEEN-AND-PAWN ENDINGS, THE
SUPERIOR KING CAN HELP WEAVE
A MATING NET AGAINST THE
DEFENDING KING.

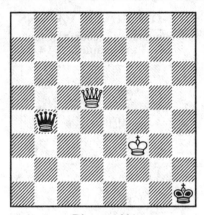

Diagram 391

Here White threatens mate in two, starting with one of two discovered checks—Kf2+ or Kg3+. Black has a choice of moves. But due to the power of the discovered check and the poor position of his king, all Black's choices lead to forced mate!

If 2. ... Kh2, then 3. Qh5+ Kg1 4. Qg5+ Kf1 5. Qg2+, and 6. Qe2 mate.

Also losing is 2. ... Qb2 3. Kg3+, or 2. ... Qc3+ 3. Kf2+. If Black tries 2. ... Qh4, then 3. Qd1+ Kh2 4. Qe2+. Finally, if 2. ...Qe1, then 3. Qh5+ Kg1 4. Qg4+.

If the threat of perpetual check is not available, the defender should resort to pinning the pawn. Here again, pins on the diagonals are usually most effective. The defender's queen has more opportunities to check or create another pin on the pawn after his opponent frees himself from a diagonal pin.

Although it is easier for a king to hide from the checks when more pawns for each side are on the board, our rules regarding checks and pins generally hold true as well for positions with a few additional pawns. In such endings, how far the passed pawn has advanced is very important. The far-advanced passed pawn is usually more important than material losses or gains.

QUEENS AND MULTIPLE PAWNS

RUBINSTEIN—CAPABLANCA
ST. PETERSBURG, 1914

Diagram 392
Black to move

Because White has an extra pawn, and because his king is protected from the checks, he has a good chance to win. In a search for salvation, Capablanca tries to create a passed pawn.

1. ... b4 2. Qxc5?

Capa's attempt pays off. White allows Black to implement his plan. The response 2. cxb4 was likewise not satisfactory because after 2. ... Qxb4 3. Qxa6 c4, Black's strong, passed c-pawn forces White to take a draw by perpetual check. But White missed the strong and logical move 2. c4!, after which Black would not be able to create a passed pawn so easily.

Diagram 393
After 2. c4!

For example: 2. ... Qa7 (with the idea a6-a5-a4) 3. Qd8+ Kh7 4. Qa5! g6 5. g3 Kg7 6. Kf1 Kh7 7. Ke2 Kg7 8. Qd8 Qb7 (or 8. ... a5 9. Kd2!) 9. Qd6 Qa7 10. Kd2 a5 11. Kc2.

Diagram 394
After 11. Kc2

Thus limiting Black's possibilities on the queenside, White is ready to press his advantage on the kingside. Promising for him, for example, would be advancing the g- and h-pawns to create passed pawns—and even mating threats. But having missed 2. c4!, White no longer has the upper hand. Let's go back to the game.

IN QUEEN ENDINGS, PERPETUAL CHECK IS NORMALLY THE BEST, AND OFTEN THE ONLY, DEFENSE. AS A GENERAL RULE, CHECKS ON THE DIAGONALS ARE MORE EFFECTIVE THAN CHECKS ON THE RANKS AND FILES.

IN QUEEN ENDINGS, A FAR-ADVANCED
PASSED PAWN IS GENERALLY MORE
IMPORTANT THAN THE GAIN OR LOSS
OF A PAWN OR EVEN SEVERAL PAWNS.

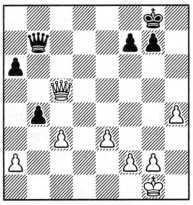

Diagram 395

2. ... bxc3 3. Qxc3 Qb1+ 4. Kh2 Qxa2

So Capa gets his passed pawn in this line as well.

5. Qc8+ Kh7 6. Qf5+ g6 7. Qf6 a5 8. g4 a4 9. h5

IF PERPETUAL CHECKS AREN'T
POSSIBLE, THE DEFENDER SHOULD
PIN THE PASSED PAWN. THE PIN ON
A DIAGONAL IS USUALLY MORE
EFFECTIVE THAN OTHER PINS.

Master of the Endgame
José Capablanca

Place of Birth: Havana, Cuba
Date of Birth: November 19, 1888

Called the greatest natural player that ever lived, "Capa" was certainly one of the best endgame players of all time. Handsome and charming, he seemed to climb the Mount Olympus of chess without too much effort. He studied little and enjoyed a celebrity life.

Defeating Lasker in 1921 to become the third world champion, he lost his title to Alekhine in 1927. The two never came to an agreement about conditions for a rematch.

Capa's natural-looking play tended to make chess look simple. But the disarming, apparent simplicity of his play was a sign of his genius. He liked to have everything under control, steering his games clear of wild complications so that his great superiority in the endgame could tell.

During one 10-year stretch, Capablanca lost only one game. Indeed, during his whole career, he was never checkmated. Of the 29 strong tournaments he played in during his career, he won or shared first in 15 and scored nine second-place finishes.

Capablanca died on March 8, 1942, after a heart attack sustained at the Manhattan Chess Club.

At one point considered nearly invincible

The first great chess idol, known to millions of nonplayers

◆ World Champion from 1921 to 1927

◆ The quintessential "natural" player who didn't study openings and yet left a legacy of opening variations named after him

◆ Known as "the chess machine"

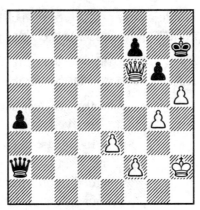

Diagram 396

9. ... gxh5!

Even after 9. ... a3 10. h6 Qb2 11. Qxf7+ Kxh6 12. Kh3 g5, White has nothing more than perpetual check.

10. Qf5+

Not 10. gxh5? Qe6!, and now Black is better!

10. ... Kg7 11. Qg5+ Kh7 12. Qxh5+

And White checks to escape with a draw.

Diagram 397

With the superior side's king protected from checks, the passed pawn is easily promoted—unless opposed by both enemy king and queen.

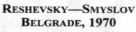

RESHEVSKY—SMYSLOV
BELGRADE, 1970

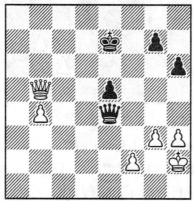

Diagram 398
White to move

1. Qc5+ Ke6 2. Qc8+

An exposed Black king lets White improve his queen's position with checks.

2. ... Kf7 3. Qd7+ Kg8 4. b5

It becomes obvious that the pawn is unstoppable because Black cannot harass White's king.

4. ... Qc2 5. Qd5+ Kh7 6. Kg2 e4 7. Qd4 Kg8 8. b6 Qb3 9. Qc5.

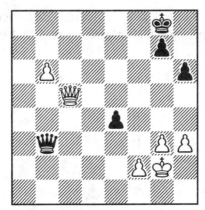

Diagram 399

White's idea is to play 10. Qc8+ and 11. b7.

9. ... Qb2 10. Qc6 Kf7

If 10. ... e3, then 11. Qe6+ and 12. Qxe3.

11. h4 g6

Or 11. ... e3 12. Qf3+.

12. Qc7+ Ke6 13. Qh7

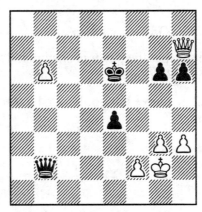

Diagram 400

13. ... Qf6

Black loses his queen immediately to an "x-ray" attack after 13. ... Qxb6 14. Qxg6+.

14. Qxh6 Qf3+ 15. Kg1, Black resigns.

When the stronger side's king can't easily hide from checks, he can be forced to make long sojourns across the board. In such cases, the duties of a wandering king are two-fold and paradoxical. On one hand, the king has to escape checks. On the other hand, he has to become a combatant and move into the fray— to attack the opponent's pawns, to support a friendly passed pawn, or even to create a threat to the opponent's king.

- ♚ The king has to escape checks.

- ♚ The king has to move into the fray—to attack the opponent's pawns, to support a friendly passed pawn, or to threaten the opponent's king.

**DLUGY—BENJAMIN
NEW YORK, 1988**

Diagram 401
Black to move

1. ... Qa2 2. Qd3! Kg7 3. Kc5 Qa5+ 4. Kc6 Kh6 5. Qb5 Qc3+ 6. Qc5

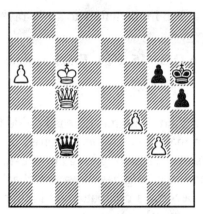

Diagram 402

6. ... Qf6+

If 6. ... Qxg3? 7. Qg5+!.

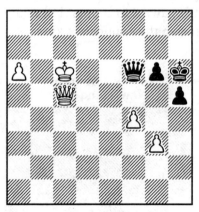

Diagram 403

7. Qd6 Qf5

If 7. ... Qc3+, then 8. Kd7 Qg7+ 9. Ke8 (the king closes in on the queen!) 9. ... Qg8+ 10. Qf8+, winning.

8. a7 Qe4+ 9. Kc7 Qc4+ 10. Kd8 Qg8+ 11. Ke7!

Diagram 404

Besides pushing the passed a-pawn toward its queening square, White has another effective plan—to exchange queens in a way that leaves him with a winning pawn ending. Such is the case after 11. ... Qg7+ 12. Ke8 Qxa7 13. Qf8+ Qg7 (or 13. ... Kh7 14. Qf7+) 14. Qxg7+ Kxg7 15. Ke7 Kh6 16. Kf6 Kh7 17. Kf7 Kh6 18. Kg8.

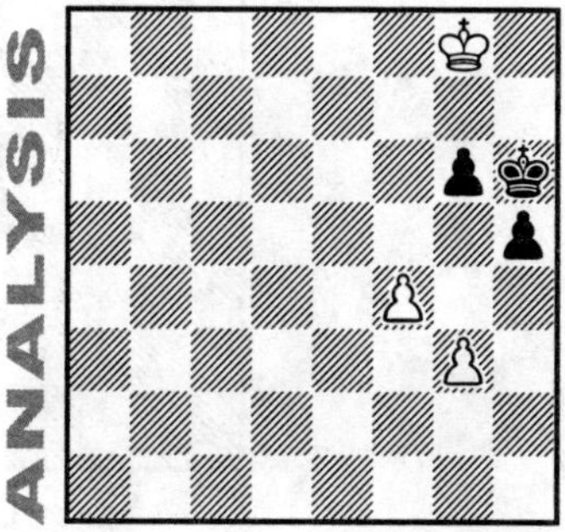

Diagram 405
After 18. Kg8 c4!

Black is in zugswang. He must play 18. ... g5, when White wins with 19. f5, and the pawn queens just in time. Returning to Diagram 404, Black plays to avoid a dead-lost pawn ending.

11. ... Qa8

IN QUEEN ENDINGS, THE DUTIES OF THE
STRONGER SIDE'S WANDERING KING ARE
TWO-FOLD AND PARADOXICAL:

♚ HE HAS TO ESCAPE CHECKS.

♚ HE HAS TO MOVE INTO THE FRAY—TO ATTACK THE ENEMY
PAWNS, TO SUPPORT A FRIENDLY PASSED PAWN,
OR TO THREATEN THE OPPONENT'S KING.

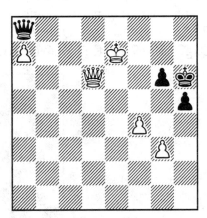

Diagram 406

**12. Qd4 Qb7+ 13. Qd7 Qb4+ 14. Kf7 Qc4+ 15. Kf8
Qc5+ 16. Kg8, Black resigns.**

Diagram 407

White threatens mate. If Black tries to keep checking with 16. ... Qc4+ 17. Qf7 Qc8+, the counter-check 18. Qf8+ forces the exchange of queens.

It is important to note that a transition into a favorable king-and-pawn ending is often created with a long "trip" by the king. The following example further illustrates this point.

TRANSITION INTO A FAVORABLE KING-AND-PAWN ENDING IS OFTEN CREATED WITH A LONG "TRIP" BY THE SUPERIOR SIDE'S KING.

MAROCZY—BETBEDER
HAMBURG, 1930

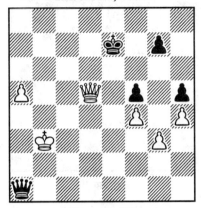

Diagram 408
Black to move

1. ... Qb1+ 2. Ka4 g6 3. a6 Qa1+ 4. Kb5 Qb2+ 5. Kc6 Qf6+ 6. Kc7.

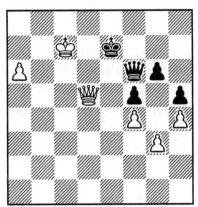

Diagram 409

White sacrifices a pawn in order to create a winning king-and-pawn ending after 6. ... Qxa6 7. Qd7+ Kf8 8. Qd6+ Qxd6+ 9. Kxd6 Kf7 10. Kd7 Kf6 11. Ke8.

6. ... Qc3+ 7. Qc6 Qe3 8. Kc8, Black resigns.

Diagram 410

If 8. ... Kf7, then 9. a7 Qxa7 10. Qd7+, when White forces the familiar and winning pawn ending.

Summary: Queens on the nearly empty board of endgames can be extremely mobile. A defending queen poses a constant threat of drawing by means of perpetual check. Usually, checking is the best defense. In most of these cases, diagonal checks are more effective than checks on the ranks and files. When checks are not available, the defender should pin the dangerous passer to its king, and the diagonal pin is generally to be preferred. The superior side can (1) threaten to exchange queens with a counter check; (2) use his king to approach his passed pawn and use it for shelter from checks; (3) paradoxically advance his king right at the enemy queen to restrict her mobility. In endings with queens and multiple pawns, a far-advanced pawn is generally more important that the gain or loss of a pawn or even several pawns. At times the superior king can even help weave a mating net against his fellow monarch. Often, a long trip by the superior king helps achieve the transition to a favorable king-and-pawn ending.

Queen Endings
Learning Exercises

Diagram 411
White to move

Diagram 412
White to move

Diagram 413
White to move

Diagram 414
White to move

Diagram 415
Black to move

Diagram 416
White to move

Queen Endings
Solutions

No. 1   **1. Qg4!** (White's queen takes up a post that prevents meaningful moves by Black.) **1. ... Kb3 2. Ke8 +-** (White breaks the pin and is ready to queen.)

No. 2   **1. Qc3** (White's queen prevents check to her king. At the same time, Her Majesty sets up potential mates on both g7 and c8. Black's queen is overloaded. **1. ... Qb7 2. Qa1 +-** (Zugzwang! Black must move, but doesn't have a new spot from which to guard both g7 and a8.)

No. 3   **1. Qc7 Qf3 2. b7 Qf8+ 3. Ka4 Qe8+ 4. Kb3 Qe3+ 5. Qc3.**

No. 4   **1. h6+ Kg6** (1. ... Kxh6 2. f5+ Kg7 3. f6+ leads to mate) **2. Qd6+ Kf5 3. Qf6+ Ke4 4. Qc6+ Kxf4 5. Qxf3+ Kxf3** (Material is even, but White has forced the queen exchange in a way that leaves Black's king fatally removed from his vulnerable pawns.) **6. Kg5 Ke4 7. Kf6 Kd5 8. Kg7 +-.**

No. 5   **1. ... e1(N)!** (Remember, promotion requires making a choice! If Black is too automatic in choosing the normally most powerful piece, he misses a win—1. ... e1(Q) 2. Qc4+ Qfe2 3. Qf4+ perpetual check.) **2. Qc4+ Qe2 3. Qf4+ Nf3+! 4. Qxf3 Qxf3 5. gxf3 Kf2 -+.** (Once again, the exchanges have lead to a materially even, but hopelessly lost pawn ending for Black.)

No. 6   **1. Ka3!** (White takes advantage of the fact his pawns are log-jammed. The attempt to create an alternative stalemate with 1. Ka1? loses to 1. ... a6.) **1. ... a6** (1. ... Kh6 2. Qc1+ Kh7 3. Qc2, returning to the same position) **2. Qb1 Qxb1, stalemate.**

Chapter 9: Mixed Bags
Some Important Ideas to Look For

◆ White wins by creating weaknesses in Black's pawn structure and by restricting the knight.

See Diagram 425.

◆ White's pawn is too far advanced to win.

See Diagram 430.

◆ For the queen to prevail, White must drive the Black rook away from its king.

See Diagram 447.

◆ Encamped in a solid fortress, Black holds, even with a material disadvantage.

See Diagram 463.

Chapter 9
Mixed Bags:
Rook Against Minor Pieces;
Queen Against Various Pieces

mbalance on the chessboard gives at once the most interesting and the most difficult-to-evaluate situations, regardless of the phase of the game. Suppose a top center and a guard play basketball against two high-scoring forwards. Or suppose two karate experts spar

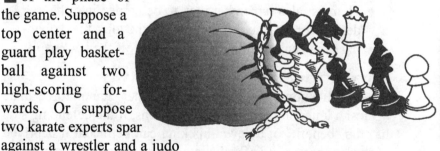

against a wrestler and a judo master. The possibilities are complicated. But once again, at least on the chessboard, a few key positions and general principles will see the practical player through nearly any challenge he faces.

BASIC CHECKMATES
We won't give some very basic knowledge here, such as the basic checkmating methods against the lone king. These techniques are available in the early volumes of the *Comprehensive*

Chess Course. We will reiterate that it is very easy to mate with queen or rook. Likewise, it is simple to mate with the two bishops. Additionally, it's useful to review briefly the basic ideas of some more complex situations.

BISHOP AND KNIGHT

It is difficult, but possible, to force mates with bishop and knight. But this ending is very rare—indeed, you may never have the position during your entire life. It's enough to keep in mind four points.

- ♚ The superior side starts by pushing the weaker side to the edge of the board.

- ♚ He then pushes him into a corner of the board controlled by the bishop and delivers checkmate.

- ♚ The superior side must keep in mind that there's no way to prevent the defending king from first running to the wrong corner.

- ♚ He must also remember that, to be herded into the deadly corner (the difficult part of the job), the defending king can be temporarily allowed off the back rank.

TWO KNIGHTS AGAINST A PAWN

It's a well known irony that two knights cannot force mate against a lone king, but in some positions, if the defending side has the "benefit" of a pawn, his king can be mated if deprived of the key possibility of stalemate. In the famous Troitzky position at right, White to play mates in six: 1. Nc4 a3 2. Ne5 a2 3. Ng6+ Kh7 4. Nf8+ Kh8 5. Nh4 (Black would be stalemated, except he's forced (!) to promote his pawn) 5. ... a1(Q) 6. Nh4-g6, checkmate.

TROITZKY

Diagram 417
White to move

FOCUS ON PRACTICALITY

The ending with two bishops against knight has been proven to be a win, albeit a very difficult one, even for a GM. But, like bishop and knight against lone king, once again, you're not likely to ever have to play such an endgame. For the non-grand-master, there are lots of more useful topics to spend time on! Let's move on to more practical situations.

ROOK VERSUS KNIGHT WITH NO PAWNS ON THE BOARD

It's natural for the superior side to want to make use of his extra muscle to push the weaker side's forces to the edge of the board to limit their mobility and increase his advantage. In the endings with the rook against the knight, the weaker side is not in any particular danger when pushed up against the rim of the board—but danger lurks in the corners.

> *Properly taught, a student can learn more in a few hours than*
> *he would find out in ten years of untutored trial and error.*
> *—World Champion Emanuel Lasker*

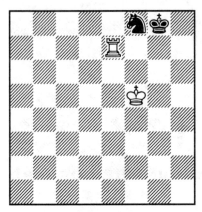

Diagram 418
White to move

1. Kf6 Nh7+

Moving the king with 1. ... Kh8 is bad because of 2. Re8 Kg8 3. Rd8.

2. Kg6 Nf8+ 3. Kh6 Kh8 4. Rf7 Kg8!

If 4. ... Ne6?, then 5. Rf6, winning.

5. Rg7+ Kh8 6. Rg1

Diagram 419

It may seem that White is winning. For example 6. ... Nh7 7.

Kg6 Kg8 (7. ... Nf8+ 8. Kf7 Nh7 9. Rg8#) 8. Rg2 Nf8+ 9.
Kf6+ followed by 10. Kf7; or 6. ... Ne6 7. Kg6 Nf8+ 8. Kf7.
But Black saves himself with ...

6. ... Nd7!, draw.

Now if 7. Kg6, then 7. ... Kg8 8. Rg2 Kf8 or 8. Rd1 Nf8+.

DON'T STAND IN THE CORNER!

In the old days, if you made a dumb mistake, your school-
teacher might have made you stand in the corner. Here, stand-
ing in the corner is itself the mistake. In Diagram 418, shift the
Black army just one square, to the very corner of the board, and
it's a different story. It's easy to see that the following two positions are lost for Black no matter who is to move.

Diagram 420   **Diagram 421**
White or Black to move, Black is "cornered" and lost.

**THE LESSON IS CLEAR:
IF YOU HAVE THE KNIGHT, STAY OUT
OF THE CORNER!**

In general, the knight should try to stay near its king. Otherwise, it could be cut off and captured.

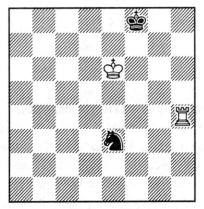

Diagram 422
White to move

1. Re4 Nd1

If 1. ... Ng2, the rook corrals the knight, which has to stay put while White plays 2. Kf6, winning the horseman. If 1. ... Nc2, then 2. Kd5 Na3 3. Kc5 Nb1 4. Kb4 Nd2 5. Rf4+ Ke7 6. Kc3 Nb1+ 7. Kb2 Nd2 8. Kc2, with the win.

2. Rf4+ Kg7 3. Rf3

The knight is cut off from its king. Now it's time to trap it.

3. ... Kg6

Or 3. ... Nb2 4. Kd5 Kg6 5. Kd4 Kg5 6. Rf1 Kg4 7. Rb1 Na4 8. Rb4.

4. Ke5 Kg5 5. Kd4 Kg4 6. Rf1 Nb2 7. Rb1 Na4 8. Rb4, winning.

A USEFUL, KNIGHT-TRAPPING IDEA:
PUT YOUR ROOK A BISHOP'S MOVE, WITH
ONE SQUARE INTERVENING, FROM THE
KNIGHT. IN THIS FORMATION, THE ROOK
TAKES THE MAXIMUM NUMBER OF SQUARES
FROM THE KNIGHT. *(FOR EXAMPLE, A
BLACK KNIGHT ON G2 IS FULLY CUT
OFF BY A WHITE ROOK ON E4).*

Diagram 423
White to move

ROOK VERSUS KNIGHT WITH PAWNS ON THE BOARD

With pawns on the board, the stronger side usually wins if he
can limit the knight's movement. Statistically, the more pawns
the merrier for the stronger side. The defender, as one would
expect, is better off when all the pawns are on the same side of
the board.

SZABO—TRIFUNOVIC
STOCKHOLM, 1948

Diagram 424
White to move

1. Ke5 Nh7 2. Rc6 Kf8

Now the White pawns attack to create weaknesses in Black's pawn structures.

3. f4 Kg7 4. Rd6 Nf8 5. g4 Nh7

5. ... Ne6? 6. Rxe6 fxe6 7. Kxe6 +-.

6. h4

Diagram 425

6. ... Nf8

Or 6. ... f6+ 7. Ke6 Nf8+ 8. Ke7 Nh7 9. h5 +-.

7. f5 gxf5 8. gxf5 h5 9. Rd1 Nh7 10. Rg1+

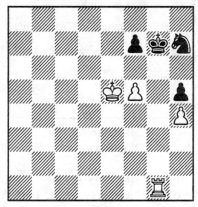

Diagram 426

10. ... Kh8.

Or 10. ... Kf8 11. f6 Ke8 12. Rg8+ Kd7 13. Rg7 +-.

11. Kd6, Black resigns.

ROOK VERSUS BISHOP

The ending with rook against bishop usually ends in a draw. Once again, pushing the defending side to the edge of the board is not dangerous for him. In fact here the weaker side can even run to a corner—but only to half of them!

Diagram 427
White to move

This is an important position to remember. The Black king is located at the safe corner. It's easy to see that White's attempts to strengthen his position, such as 1. Ra8, lead to a stalemate. Black holds easily.

1. Ra5 Bh7+ 2. Kf6 Bg8 3. Rh5+ Bh7 4. Rh2

Or 4. Kf7 stalemate.

4. ... Kg8 5. Ra2 Kh8, etc.

The following position demonstrates what happens when the defending king runs to the wrong-color corner square.

THE WEAKER SIDE IN ROOK VERSUS BISHOP ENDINGS CAN RETREAT HIS KING TO A CORNER SQUARE UNREACHABLE BY HIS BISHOP.

Diagram 428
Black to move

1. ... Bg1

Forced. If 1. ... Bc5, then 2. Rc7 Bd6 3. Rc8+ Bf8 4. Re8, winning. Here the pin works!

2. Rf1 Bh2 3. Rf2 Bg3

3. ... Bg1 4. Rg2 Bb6 5. Rb2+-.

4. Rg2 Bd6

If 4. ... Bf4, White plays 5. Kf5+ or 4. ... Bh4 5. Kh5+.

5. Rd2 Be7 6. Ra2 Bb4

If 6. ... Kf8, then 7. Ra8+.

7. Ra8+ Bf8 8. Rc8 Kh8 9. Rxf8 mate.

ROOK AND PAWN VERSUS BISHOP

Usually, rook and pawn versus bishop win easily, but there are some important exceptions.

Diagram 429
White to move

If White's pawn were still on g5, 1. Kg6 would win easily. Now to win, White must be creative.

1. g7! Kh7

1. ... Bxg7 is bad because of 2. Kg6 Be5 3. Re7.

2. Rf7!

If 2. g8(Q)+ Kxg8 3. Kg6, then 3. ... Kf8—and Black's king gets out of the "bad" corner.

2. ... Bd4

2. ... Bxg7 3. Kg5 Kg8 4. Kg6.

3. g8(Q)+ Kxg8 4. Kg6, winning.

We've reached the winning position in Diagram 428. But what if all the pieces in Diagram 429 were shifted one square to the left?

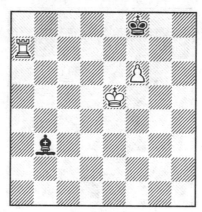

Diagram 430
White to move

Here the position is a draw.

HERE'S THE MORAL FOR THE SIDE WITH THE PASSED PAWN: DON'T RUSH TO PUSH YOUR PAWN; LEAD WITH YOUR KING.

Diagram 431
White to move

Once again, if White's pawn were still on f5, White would win easily, while the pawn sac, successful in the last example, doesn't work. After 1. f7 Kg7! 2. Re7 Ba2 3. f8(Q)+ Kxf8 4. Kf6 Kg8, Black's king gets free. White's attempts to win without sacrificing a pawn, and instead occupying e6 or g6 with his king and threatening mate, also fail. For example:

1. Rc7 Bd5

But not 1. ... Bb3? 2. Kg6.

2. Rc5 Ba2 3. Rb5 Bc4! 4. Rb4 Bd5 5. Kg6 Bf7+ 6. Kf5 Bd5 7. Ke5 Ba2, draw.

ROOK AND PAWNS VERSUS BISHOP AND PAWNS

When both sides have pawns, the main winning method is the penetration by the stronger side's king.

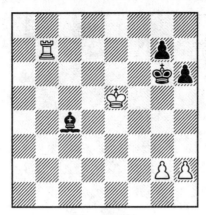

Diagram 432
White to move

1. Kd6

The king tries for the f8-square.

1. ... Kf6 2. Rb4 Ba2 3. Rf4+ Kg5 4. g3!

The great positioning of the White rook yields Black no counterplay.

4. ... Bb1 5. Ke7

WHEN EACH SIDE HAS SEVERAL PAWNS, THE ROOK BEATS THE BISHOP OR THE KNIGHT IN THE MAJORITY OF CASES. THE DEFENDER HAS HIS BEST CHANCES WHEN ALL THE PAWNS ARE LOCATED ON ONE SIDE OF THE BOARD. AND, AS USUAL, THE MORE PAWNS, THE LIKELIER THE WIN.

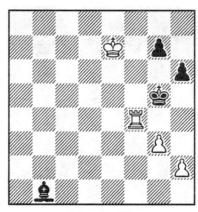

Diagram 433

5. ... h5

If 5. ... g6, then 6. Kf8 h5 7. Kg7, with the threat of 8. h4 mate.

6. Kf8 Kh6 7. Rb4 Bd3 8. Kg8 Bc2 9. Rb6+

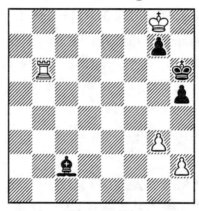

Diagram 434

9. ... g6

With Black's pawns fixed on the color of his bishop, White easily penetrates and wins.

10. h4 Bf5 11. Kf7 Bc2 12. Kf6 Bf5 13. Rb8 Kh7 14. Kg5 Kg7 15. Rb7+

Diagram 435

15. ... Kg8 16. Kf6 and 17. Rg7 and 18. Rxg6, with the win.

In this type of ending, the defender often, but not always, wants his own pawns on the opposite-color squares than those covered by his bishop, in order to try to prevent dangerous penetration by his opponent's king.

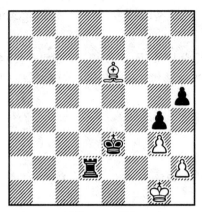

Diagram 436
White to move

1. Bc8 Rb2

With the threat of 2. ... Kf3.

2. Be6 Ke4 3. Bc4 Rb4 4. Be6 Ke5 5. Bc8 Kf6 6. Bd7 Rb2 7. Bc8 Kg5

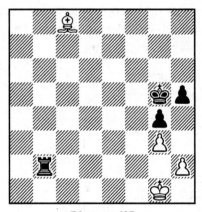

Diagram 437

8. Ba6

It is necessary to counter the future appearance of Black's king on h3 with Bf1+.

8. ... h4 9. gxh4+

Otherwise, 9. ... h3 would later allow dangerous mating threats.

> **9. ... Kxh4 10. Bc4 Kh3 11. Bf1+ Kh4**
> **12. Ba6 g3 13. hxg3+ Kxg3 14. Kf1, draw.**

ROOK AND BISHOP VERSUS ROOK

For non-masters, there are only three things to keep in mind for practical play:

- ♚ These endings are rare—you can play your whole life without encountering one;
- ♚ They're extremely difficult for both sides, and on a GM level the practical chances of winning are 50-50;
- ♚ Both sides must be persistent—the weaker side should be alert and the stronger side, creative.

We give the positions below for the curious. The purely practical can skip to the next section, "Queen versus rook."

COMPUTERS HAVE SHOWN THAT ROOK AND BISHOP VERSUS ROOK ENDGAMES CAN SOMETIMES REQUIRE, EVEN WITH BEST PLAY, AN EXTENSION TO THE "FIFTY-MOVE" RULE. THE DEFENDERS SHOULD KEEP AN ACCURATE SCORE SHEET AND CLAIM THE DRAW AS SOON AS IT'S LEGAL. (SEE CHAPTER 8, QUEEN ENDINGS, FOR RULES.)

PHILIDOR

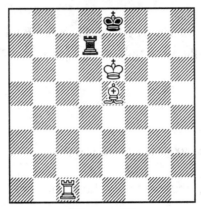

Diagram 438
White to move

Even in a winning position, the way to victory is very complex, but so is the defense! Black's king has been pushed back to the edge. Now White tries to force his opponent's rook to leave the seventh rank.

1. Rc8+

Not 1. Bf6? Re7+.

1. ... Rd8 2. Rc7 Rd2 3. Rb7 Rd1 4. Rg7 Rf1

On 4. ... Kf8 5. Rh7 Rg1 6. Ra7 +-.

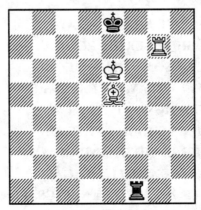

Diagram 439

5. Bg3 Rf3

The best. If 5. ... Kf8, then 6. Rg4 Ke8 7. Ra4 Rd1 8. Bh4 Kf8 9. Bf6 Re1+ 10. Be5 Kg8 11. Rh4 +-.

6. Bd6 Re3+ 7. Be5 Rf3 8. Re7+ Kf8

If 8. ... Kd8, then 9. Rb7—and Black doesn't have 9. ... Rc3. That's why the Black rook was invited to the third rank.

9. Rc7 Kg8 10. Rg7+ Kf8 11. Rg4

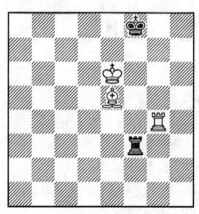

Diagram 440

11. ... Ke8

Or 11. ... Re3 12. Rh4.

12. Bf4 Kf8 13. Bd6+ Ke8 14. Rg8+, winning.

With best play, the weaker side can hold in most positions, at least in theory.

FLOHR—RESHEVSKY
ZEMMERING, 1937

Diagram 441
Black to move

1. ... Kd8!

Taking up a position in front of the opponent's king, but at a distance of two squares.

2. Rh7 Rd2 3. Ke5 Kc8

Black's king correctly goes to the opposite side of the board from his opposing monarch!

4. Bc5 Rd7

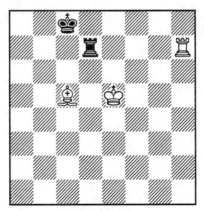

Diagram 442

5. Be7 Kb7 6. Ke6 Kc6 7. Rh1 Rd2
8. Rc1+ Kb5 9. Bd6 Re2+ 10. Kd7 Re4 11. Rc5+

Diagram 443

11. ... Ka4 12. Kc6 Kb3 13. Kd5 Re8 14. Rb5+ Kc2
15. Bc5 Kd3 16. Rb3+ Ke2 17. Bd4 Rd8+ 18. Ke4
Re8+ 19. Be5 Ke1

Diagram 444

We're back to nearly the starting position, except that the board has been "flipped" from top to bottom! White can't make meaningful progress. It's a draw.

QUEEN VERSUS ROOK

The powerful queen usually wins against the rook, but not without toil. The position below is a "generic" one, widely applicable.

Diagram 445
White to move

White has a two-step plan:

- ♚ Push the opponent's pieces to the edge of the board.
- ♚ Split up his opponent's rook and king, putting distance between them, and win the rook with a fork.

1. Kb2 Rf4 2. Kc3 Re4 3. Kd3 Rd4+ 4. Ke3 Rd5 5. Qg3+ Kf5 6. Qf4+ Ke6 7. Ke4 Rd6 8. Qf5+ Ke7 9. Ke5 Rd7 10. Qf6+ Ke8

Fact: After becoming world champion, Bobby Fischer turned down millions of dollars in endorsement fees because he didn't feel the products were the best in their fields.

Diagram 446

The first part of the plan is accomplished. Now, White must avoid the trap 11. Ke6? Rd6+ 12. Kxd6 stalemate!

11. Qh8+ Kf7 12. Qh7+ Ke8 13. Qg8+ Ke7 14. Qc8

Diagram 447

White needs to separate his opponent's pieces.

14. ... Rd1

14. ... Rd8 15. Qe6+ Kf8 16. Kf6 or 14. ... Rd3 15. Qe6+ Kd8 16. Qg8+ Kc7 17. Qc4+.

15. Qc5+ Kd8 16. Qa5+ Ke7 17. Qb4+ Kd8 18. Ke6!

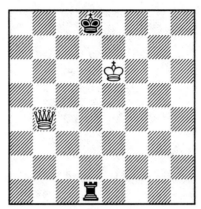

Diagram 448

**18. ... Kc7 19. Qf4+ Kc8 20. Qc4+ Kd8
21. Qb3 Re1+ 22. Kd6, winning.**

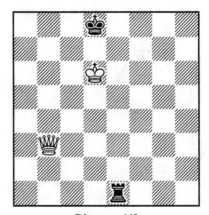

Diagram 449
White to move

22. ... Kc8 23. Qc3+, winning the rook, or 22. ... Ke8
23. Qg8 mate.

QUEEN VERSUS ROOK
AND NON-ROOK PAWN

If the defender has a pawn on his second rank, and it's not a rook's pawn, he can reach a draw by building a fortress.

Diagram 450
White to move

1. Qh7 Ke8 2. Qg8+ Kd7 3. Qh8 Rd6 4. Kf5 Rf6+ 5. Ke5 Rd6, draw.

White's king can't penetrate, and his queen has no room to attack from behind, while Black's rook has two good squares to shuffle between. (Therefore there is no threat of zugzwang.) Black holds the draw.

QUEEN VERSUS ROOK
AND ROOK PAWN

With a rook pawn on his second rank, the weaker side can work from only one safe square for the rook and loses to zugzwang.

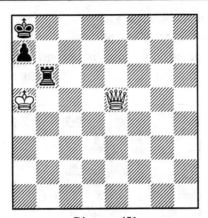

Diagram 451
White to move

1. Qd5+ Kb8 2. Qd7

Zugzwang!

2. ... Rh6

If 2. ... Ka8, then 3. Qc8+ Rb8 4. Qc6+ Rb7 5. Ka6.

3. Qe8+ Kc7 4. Qf7+, winning.

On the next move, Black loses either his rook or his pawn.

Let's move all the pieces in Diagram 451 one rank "down."

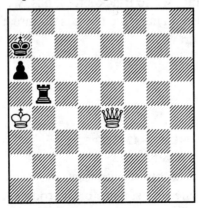

Diagram 452
White to move

Now Black has more room to maneuver and draws.

Master of the Endgame
Emanuel Lasker

Place of Birth: Berlinchen, Prussia
Date of Birth: December 24, 1868

Emanuel Lasker was world champion from 1894 to 1921. Famous for his will to win and his fighting spirit, his dedication was not to any set of theories or school of chess thought, but to the "struggle" itself.

Second Official Chess World Champion

Top-finisher at major international tournaments from the early 1890s to 1936—at the age of 67!

◆ One of the greatest defensive players of all time

◆ Author of *Common Sense in Chess* and *Lasker's Manual of Chess*

◆ First to work to increase fees for champions

◆ Vanquisher of Mieses, Bird, Blackburne, Steinitz, Tarrasch, Marshall, Janowski.

Some of his contemporaries accused Lasker of making bad moves on purpose to confuse his opponents! It is probably closer to the truth that he tried to go down unfamiliar paths, thereby at times getting a somewhat inferior game out of the opening. Such positions gave scope to his great and original defensive abilities. In fact, in New York 1924, where he placed first ahead of Alekhine and Capablanca, Lasker rewrote endgame theory over the board by drawing against rook and pawn with a lone knight.

Later in life, he was friends with Albert Einstein. Reportedly, during their private talks, Einstein would insist on discussing chess, while Lasker would try to turn the conversation to mathematics. Lasker wrote books and papers on chess, mathematics, philosophy and bridge.

Driven out of Germany by the persecution of the Jews, he finally came to the U.S., where he died January 13, 1941.

But too much space can also be dangerous! With an already advanced non-rook pawn, the stronger side wins because he can drive the king out of his fortress from behind. (There can be drawing possibilities if the pawn is *far*-advanced.)

Diagram 453

Let's look at the typical method of winning.

1. Qb8+ Kd7 2. Qb7+ Kd8 3. Qc6 Ke7 4. Qc7+ Ke6 5. Qd8.

Diagram 454

5. ... Rf5+

Or 5. ... Rc5 6. Qe8+ Kf6 7. Qd7.

6. Kg4 Re5 7. Qe8+

Diagram 455

7. ... Kf6

Or 7. ... Kd5 8. Qc8 (zugzwang) 8. ... Re4+ 9. Kf5 Re5+ 10. Kf6 Re4 11. Qc3 Re6+ 12. Kf7 Re5 13. Kf8! Re4 14. Qd3+

Diagram 456
After 14. Qd3+

14. ... Rd4 15. Qf5+ Kc4 16. Qc2+ Kd5 17. Ke7 Ke5 18. Qe2+ Kf4 19. Kd7 Rd5 20. Kc7 Rd4 21. Kc6 (see diagram, next page)

My favorite piece is the one that wins!
                    —Anonymous

Diagram 457
After 21. Kc6

21. ... Kf5 22. Qe3, winning. Back to the actual game (Diagram 455) after 7. ... Kf6.

8. Qd7

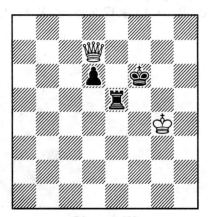

Diagram 458

8. ... Rd5 9. Kf4 Rd4+ 10. Ke3 Rd1 11. Qd8+ Kf7 12. Qh4

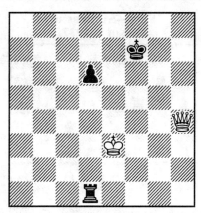

Diagram 459

White is winning because the rook has to leave the d-file. King moves invite a double attack on king and rook by the queen. If 12. ... Rd5, then White "pins and wins" with 13. Qc4. Or 12. ... Rc1 13. Kd4 Rc5 (13. ... Rd1+ 14. Ke4) 14. Qd8 Ke6 15. Qe8+ Kf6 16. Qd7, finally winning the pawn.

QUEEN VERSUS ROOK
AND MINOR PIECE

The queen is usually somewhat stronger than the rook and knight, or rook and bishop. King penetration and the creation of zugzwang are the typical methods to play for a win. The weaker side usually tries to create an impregnable fortress.

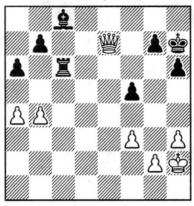

Diagram 460
White to move

So far Black has everything protected. But soon he won't be able to defend against all of his opponent's threats, which include: 1) using his queen and b-pawn to push away the rook; 2) advancing his h-pawn to h5; 3) centralizing his king.

1. b5 axb5 2. axb5 Rc4 3. h4 Rc2 4. h5 Rc4 5. Kg3

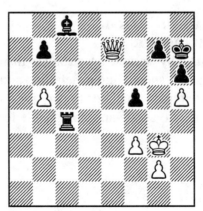

Diagram 461

5. ... Rc3

If 5. ... f4+, then 6. Kh2! (zugzwang) 6. ... Kh8 7. Qe8+ Kh7

8. Qg6+ Kh8 (or 8. ... Kg8 9. Qd6) 9. Qf7, winning the f-pawn).

**6. Qd6 Rc2 7. Qg6+ Kh8 8. Qe8+ Kh7 9. Kf4 Rc1
10. Qg6+ Kh8 11. Ke5 Bd7 12. Qb6 Bc8 13. Kd6**

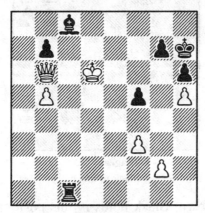

Diagram 462

White's king threatens to head for f8 in order to attack g7.

13. ... Kg8 14. Qe3, Black resigns.

His rook is forced to leave the c-file, and abandon the bishop, because 14. ... Rc2 loses to 15. g4.

Now let's take a look at queen versus rook and knight. Depending on the pawn structure, the knight can be in general a better or a worse member of the defense team than the bishop. If the pawns are on both sides of the board, the bishop is normally for choice, while if the pawns are all on one side, the knight is at least as good.

PORTISCH—MILES
TILBURG, 1981

Diagram 463
Black to move

Even a pawn down, Black holds in this position, which illustrates that the knight is quite effective when the action is on one side and there are few pawns left.

1. ... Kh8

Black intends to play 2. ... g5, creating a fortress. If 2. Qe6, then 2. ... g5! 3. Qxh6+ Rh7, with a drawn king-and-pawn ending: 4. Qh5 Rxh5+ 5. gxh5 Kh7 6. Kg3 Kg7.

2. Kg3 g5 3. Kf2 Nf7 4. Ke3 Rg8 5. Qc6 Kg7

Diagram 464

The fortress has been built.

6. f4

If 6. Ke4, Black has 6. ... Re8+, and White can't make progress—the fortress holds.

6. ... gxf4+ 7. Kxf4 Rf8 8. Qc3+ Kg6 9. Qd3+ Kf6 10. Qa6+

If White plays 10. g5+, Black has 10. ... Nxg5.

10. ... Kg7

Diagram 465

Here the rook and knight hold queen and pawn to a draw.

11. g5 Nh6+ 12. Kg3 Nf5+ 13. Kh3 Rh8+ 14. Kg4 Rf8, draw.

JAKOVICH—ZILBERSTEIN
RUSSIA, 1987

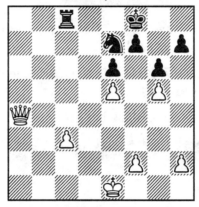

Diagram 466
White to move

Despite the weaknesses in his opponent's pawn structure, Black can't stop the c-pawn's progress, and therefore can't create a fortress, because his pieces are too passive.

1. Qd7! Ra8

Not good enough is 1. ... Rxc3. Play can continue 2. Qd8+ Kg7 3. Qxe7 Rf3 4. Ke2 Rf5 5. Kf1 Rf4 6. Kg2 Rf5 7. Kg3 h6 8. h4 followed by 9. f4, and zugzwang forces Black to part with his rook.

2. c4 Ra1+ 3. Kd2 Ra2+ 4. Kc3 Ra8 5. Kb4 Rb8+ 6. Kc5 Nf5 7. Kc6 Kg7 8. c5 Rb4 9. Kc7 Rd4 10. c6!

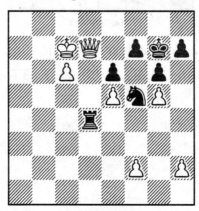

Diagram 467

10. ... Rd5 11. Kd8 Nd4 12. Ke7

If 12. c7, then 12. ... Nc6+ 13. Ke8 Rxd7 14. Kxd7 (14.
c8(Q) Re7 #) 14. ... Na7 =.

12. ... h6

If 12. ... Rxd7+ 13. cxd7 Nc6+, then 14. Kd6 Nd8 15. Kc7 +-.

13. c7, Black resigns.

Summary*: A mixture of different kinds of pieces in an endgame
creates imbalance, the hardest situation to properly evaluate.
However, as always, some general guidelines will see you
through most positions. You'll face some of the special checkmates,
like bishop and knight against lone king, rarely if ever in your
chess career, so spending a lot of time on these arcane
challenges before you reach master isn't a practical approach.*

*Rook against knight is normally a draw; the weaker side should
stay out of the corners. For the stronger side, it's a case of the
more pawns the merrier, since more pawns increase winning
chances. Rook against bishop is normally a draw. The weaker
side must stay out of the corners reachable by his bishop. Rook
and pawn against bishop usually wins. With several pawns on
the board, the ability of the king to penetrate normally
determines the outcome. Rook and bishop vs. rook is rare and
difficult—for both sides. Queen vs. rook is normally a win for
the queen but can require a lot of work. In queen vs. rook and
pawn on the second rank, if it's a non-rook pawn the weaker
side can usually draw by building a fortress. This method is not
possible for a rook pawn on the second rank—but it works if the
rook pawn is on the third rank. However, pawns on other files
advanced past the second rank fail to help build a successful
fortress, since the queen can attack from behind, and win. The
queen is usually stronger than rook and minor piece, and she
generally benefits from the presence of additional pieces and
pawns.*

Mixed Bags
Learning Exercises

Diagram 468
White to move

Diagram 469
White to move

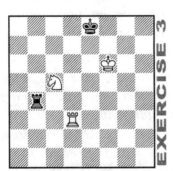

Diagram 470
White to move

Diagram 471
White to move

Diagram 472
White to move

Diagram 473
Black to move

Mixed Bags
Solutions

No. 1   **1. Kc4 a2 2. Kb3 a1(N)+ 3. Kc3 Nc2**
(3. ... Ka2 4. Rb4 Ka3 5. Rb2) **4. Re2 Na3**
(4. ... Na1 5. Rh2) **5. Kb3 +-.**

No. 2   **1. a7 Rf5+ 2. Ke2 Re5+** (2. ... Rf8 3. Bf6+ Kc5 4. Be7+)
3. Kd2 Re8 4. Bf2+ Ke5 5. Bg3+ Ke6 6. Bb8 +-.

No. 3   **1. Ne6** (it's usually relatively easy for the rook to draw against rook
and knight, but here the poor position of Black's rook allows it no
checks.) **1. ... Rb8 2. Rd1! Rc8 3. Ng7+ Kf8 4. Rg1 Rc6+** (or
4. ... Kg8 5. Ne6+ Kh7 6. Kf7 Kh6 7. Rh1#) **5. Ne6+ Ke8
6. Rg8+ Kd7 7. Rd8#.**

No. 4   **1. Bc5 Rc8** (1. ... Kc8 2. Ba7) **2. Bb6+ Ke8 3. Bc7 a5 4. Kd1 a4
5. Kc1 a3 6. Kb1 a2+ 7. Ka1 +-.**

No. 5   **1. Ra6+ Kf7 2. Kf5!** (definitely not 2. f5?), **winning.**

No. 6   **1. ... Bxg5+ 2. Kxg5 Rf6, draw.**

Multi-Piece Endings
Some Important Ideas to Look For

◆ White's bishop pair dominates the board.

See Diagram 474.

◆ Doubled rooks—"blind pigs"— dominate the play.

See Diagram 487.

◆ A spatial advantage can be overwhelming.

See Diagram 489.

◆ White's weak pawn on d4 isn't enough for Black to win, so he uses the technique of creating a second weakness.

See Diagram 495.

Chapter 10
Multi-Piece Endings:
The Middlegame of Endgames

In one sense, the more pieces on the board, the more complicated the possibilities are. Naturally, the theory of multipiece endgames is based on the simple endings we've already examined. Of course the extra pieces add an additional set of strategies.

ADVANTAGE OF THE BISHOP PAIR

In open positions, having the bishop pair against the knight and bishop (or two knights) is most often an advantage. When there are passed pawns on the board, the advantage of the two bishops is particularly apparent.

CAPABLANCA—VIDMAR
NEW YORK, 1927

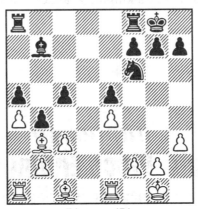

Diagram 474
White to move

The main weakness in Black's position is the pawn on a5; White is trying to get at it. Black has a hard time organizing a defense because his opponent's bishops have de facto control over the entire board.

> **1. cxb4 cxb4 2. f3 Rfd8 3. Be3 h6 4. Red1 Bc6 5. Rac1 Be8 6. Kf2 Rxd1 7. Rxd1 Rc8 8. g4**

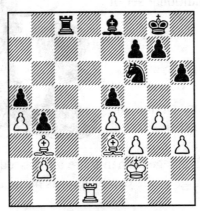

Diagram 475

White plans to follow g4 with h3-h4 and g4-g5, and after forcing the retreat of Black's knight, to attack the a5-pawn with Rd5.

8. ... Bd7 9. Bb6 Be6

It's hopeless. There's no defense. If 9. ... Ra8 10. Bc7 nets a pawn.

10. Bxe6 fxe6 11. Rd8+ Rxd8 12. Bxd8 Nd7 13. Bxa5 Nc5

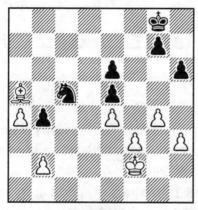

Diagram 476

14. b3 Nxb3 15. Bxb4 Nd4 16. a5, Black resigns.

TAIMANOV—SMYSLOV
TBILISI, 1967

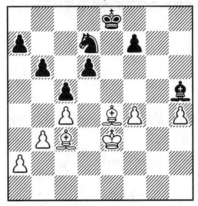

Diagram 477
White to move

In order to win, White has to advance his passed pawn. In the first stage of his plan, he strengthens his position in the center, limiting Black's mobility.

1. f5 Ne5 2. f6 Ng6 3. Be1 Nf8 4. Bg3 Kd7 5. Bf5+ Ne6 6. Bh3 Bd1 7. Bf4

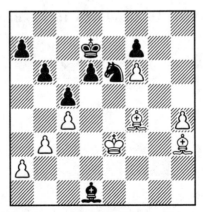

Diagram 478

White's next step is to transfer his bishop to e7, tying up Black's pieces even more.

7. ... Bh5 8. Bh6 Bd1 9. Bf8 Bh5 10. Be7 a5

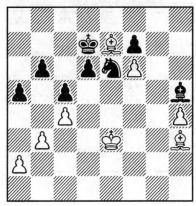

Diagram 479

An attempt to create counterplay. If Black is passive, White transfers his king to g3, plays Bg4, and wins.

11. Kf2 Bd1 12. Kg3 a4 13. bxa4 Bxa4 14. h5 Bc2 15. h6 Bg6 16. Bg4 Bh7 17. Kf2

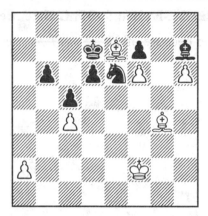

Diagram 480

Now the game is decided by the White king's penetration into the queenside.

**17. ... Bb1 18. Ke3 Bh7 19. Kd2 Bb1 20. Kc3 Be4
21. Kb3 d5**

Or 21. ... Bh7 22. Ka4 Be4 23. Kb5 +-.

22. cxd5 Bxd5+ 23. Kc3 Be4 24. Kc4 Ke8 25. Bf3!

If 25. Kb5?, then 25. ... Nd4+ 26. Kxb6 c4.

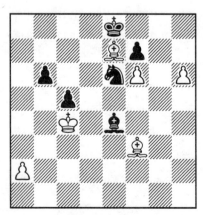

Diagram 481
After 25. Bf3!

25. ... b5+ 26. Kc3 Ng5 27. h7, Black resigns.

Black gives it up because of 27. ... Bxh7 28. Bc6, mate.

Having the two bishops is not always an advantage. The relative strength of this pair depends on the overall pawn structure and the position of the kings.

KLAVINS—RAGOZIN
RIGA, 1952

Diagram 482
White to move

In this closed position, the doubled pawns on f2 and f3 dangerously weaken White's pawn structure. White is practically in zugzwang. Black's attack on the kingside is decisive.

1. Bd1 Nf4 2. Bc2 f6 3. Kf1 Kf7 4. Bd1 Kg6 5. Bc2 Kg5 6. Bb1 Kh4 7. Bc2 Kh3 8. Kg1 h6 9. Bb1 h5 10. Bc2 Nd3

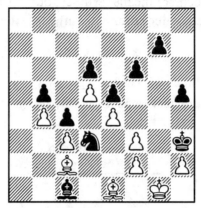

Diagram 483

11. Kf1 Kxh2 12. Ke2 Kg2, White resigns.

TWO ROOKS VERSUS TWO ROOKS
In general, the most effective base of operations for rooks is the seventh rank.

SCHLECHTER—MAROCZY
KARLSBAD, 1907

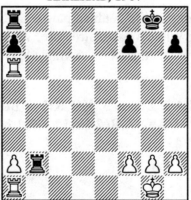

Diagram 484
Black to move

In German, "Schlechter" means "worse," but at first glance he appears to be much better here, with an extra pawn and pressure against the a-pawn that seems to nail down the Black rook to a passive position on a8. In search for salvation, Maroczy follows the principle that an active rook is generally worth a pawn.

1. ... Rd8! 2. Rxa7 Rdd2

Now White has two extra pawns, but he has to give one of them back. Black will capture the distant a-pawn to reach a rook ending with two pawns versus three on one side—a well known, easy draw.

3. Ra3 Kf8!

If 3. ... Rxf2, then 4. Rg3+ Kf8 5. a3—keeping an important pawn.

4. Rf1 Rxa2 5. Rxa2 Rxa2, draw.

The brilliant embodiment of Steinitzian theory, Carl Schlechter (1874-1918) narrowly missed winning the title in his match against Lasker. Schlechter died of starvation eight years later.

Courtesy USCF

SZABO—PORTISCH
BUDAPEST, 1959

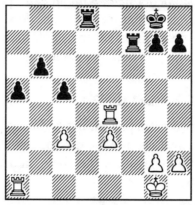

Diagram 485
Black to move

In this position Black has a number of advantages—an opportunity to capture White's second rank, an extra pawn, the distant, passed a-pawn, and a much better pawn structure than his opponent, who is saddled with two isolated pawns.

1. ... Rd2!

The fastest way to win.

2. Rb1 Rff2

The Black rooks are what Janowski called "blind pigs on the seventh" because of their tendency to devour everything they bump up against.

3. Rxb6

Or 3. Rg4 Rb2 4. Rd1 Rfd2 5. Rf1 a4 -+.

3. ... Rxg2+ 4. Kf1 Rxh2

Black threatens mate.

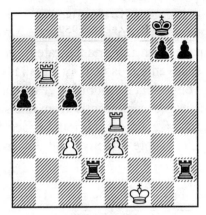

Diagram 486

5. Rb8+ Kf7 6. Rb7+ Kf6 7. Rb6+.

Or 7. Rf4+ Ke6 -+.

7. ... Kg5 8. Kg1

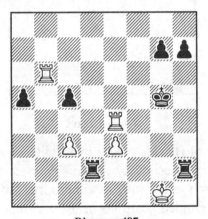

Diagram 487

**8. ... Rdg2+ 9. Kf1 Rc2 10. Kg1 Rhd2,
White resigns.**

THE IMPORTANCE OF A
SPATIAL ADVANTAGE

The fight for space is an important strategy in the multi-piece endings. A space advantage is usually a real advantage because it limits your opponent's mobility, especially when he's required to transfer pieces promptly from one side of the board to the other. And, of course, additional space frees your own pieces, making them more effective and powerful.

SMYSLOV—EUWE
WORLD CHAMPIONSHIP TOURNAMENT, 1948

Diagram 488
White to move

The restriction of Black's pieces in a limited space allows White to penetrate decisively with his dark-square bishop. Siegbert Tarrasch said it in a way appropriate to his training as physician—"Cramped positions bear the germs of defeat!"

1. Ba5! Nc8

If 1. ... Bc8, then 2. ... b4! Bg1 3. Kg2 Bd4 4. Nxd4 exd4 5. Bb6 +-.

2. Bg4!

A winning move, Black has no time to untangle his queenside pieces.

2. ... f6

Or 2. ... Ke8 3. Bc7 Ke7 4. Kg2, zugzwang.

3. Be6 fxg5 4. hxg5 Nb6

Black also falls prey to a zugzwang after 4. ... Ke8 5. Bc7 Ke7 6. Kf3.

Diagram 489

5. b4 Nc4 6. bxc5 Nxa5 7. cxd6+ Kxd6 8. Bf7 Nc4 9. Bxg6 a5 10. Kg4 b4 11. Bf5

Threatening 12. g6 Ke7 13. Kg5 Kf8 14. Kf6.

11. ... Ke7 12. Be6 Nd6 13. Ne3!

Seventh World Champion Vassily Smyslov (1921-) melded the disparate strengths of Chigorin, Nimzovitch and Alekhine into a richly original approach to openings and middlegames—made particularly deadly when combined with his endgame virtuosity.

Photo by Nigel Eddis. Courtesy USCF.

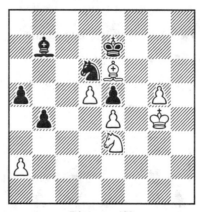

Diagram 490

13. ... Nxe4

Or 13. ... a4 14. Nf5+ Nxf5 15. exf5 b3 16. f6+ Kd6 17. f7 Ke7 18. d6+ +-.

14. Kf5 Nd6+

If Black tries 13. ... Nc3 with an eye toward ... Nxa2, not only would his short-range knight be out of touch with the critical action in the center, but after 14. Kxe5, White could push his d-pawn with check, uncovering his bishop on the a2- and b3-squares.

15. Kxe5 Nf7+ 16. Kf4 Nd8 17. Nf5+ Kf8 18. g6 Nxe6+ 19. dxe6 a4 20. Ke5, Black resigns.

ALEKHINE—FINE
KEMERI, 1937

Diagram 491
White to move

On 1. Nd4 Ne3, Black is fine. But Alekhine found a way to restrict the American champion's pieces. In the ending, the king belongs in the center—if it's safe to be there. And here White's king on d2 is safe.

1. Kd2!

Now Black has to sit tight in a cramped position in which it is difficult to coordinate his pieces.

1. ... Nb6 2. Ne3 0-0

If 2. ... Ke7, then 3. Bb4+.

3. a4 Rfd8 4. Bd3 e5 5. Rhc1 Be6 6. Rxc8 Rxc8 7. Bb4

This prevents centralization of the Black king by 7. ... Kf8.

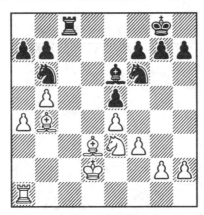

Diagram 492

7. ... Ne8

Or 7. ... Nc4+ 8. Nxc4 Bxc4 9. Rc1 Be6 10. Rxc8 Bxc8 11. Bd6 Nd7 12. a5, and White's king reaches d5 with decisive advantage.

8. a5 Nd7 9. Nd5 Bxd5 10. exd5 Nc5 11. Bf5

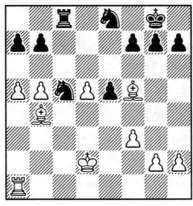

Diagram 493

11. ... Rd8

If 11. ... Nb3+, then 12. Kd3 Rd8 13. Re1 g6 14. Bh3 f6 15. Be7 +-. Whenever Black tries ... Rxd5+?, he'll get forked with Kc4.

12. Kc3! b6

On 12. ... Rxd5, White plays 13. Kc4 +-.

13. axb6 axb6 14. Bxc5 bxc5 15. b6

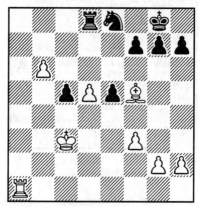

Diagram 494

15. ... Nd6 16. Bd7 Rxd7

If 16. ... Kf8, then 17. Bc6 Rb8 18. b7 (or 18. Ra8), winning.

17. Ra8+, Black resigns.

CREATING ADDITIONAL WEAKNESSES

In many positions, the existence of one weakness in your opponent's camp (for instance, a weak pawn, or your own strong passer, which counts as a weakness for your opponent) is by itself not enough for you to force a win. To be victorious, the stronger side must try to saddle his opponent with an additional weakness, creating problems that are too much for the defense to bear.

EM. LASKER—CAPABLANCA
WORLD CHAMPIONSHIP MATCH, 1921

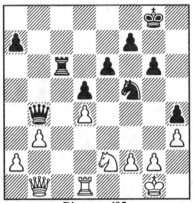

Diagram 495
Black to move

White's pieces are tied up by the defense of his isolated pawn on d4. Black can't use this weakness right away. So he plans to create a second weakness by isolating another White pawn—on the queenside.

1. ... a5

With an idea of advancing ... a5-a4.

2. Qb2 a4 3. Qd2 Qxd2 4. Rxd2 axb3 5. axb3 Rb6

Diagram 496

The queen exchange does not provide White any relief. Because of the second weak pawn, the White defense is now much more difficult.

6. Rd3 Ra6 7. g4

The idea of this last move is to force the Black knight from its wonderful post on f5. But the drawback is that White is left with a pawn-naked second rank and yields a permanent weakness on the e4 square.

7. ... hxg3 e.p. 8. fxg3

Or 8. Nxg3 Ra1+ 9. Kg2 Nd6 and 10. ... Rb1-+.

8. ... Ra2 9. Nc3 Rc2 10. Nd1 Ne7 11. Ne3 Rc1+ 12. Kf2 Nc6 13. Nd1 Rb1!

The decisive follow-through.

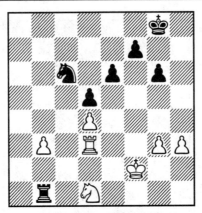

Diagram 497

14. Ke2

Better is 14. Ke1, but even in this case, Black would be winning after 14. ... Na5.

> **14. ... Rxb3 15. Ke3 Rb4 16. Nc3 Ne7 17. Ne2 Nf5+**
> **18. Kf2 g5 19. g4 Nd6 20. Ng1 Ne4+ 21. Kf1 Rb1+**
> **22. Kg2 Rb2+ 23. Kf1 Rf2+ 24. Ke1 Ra2**

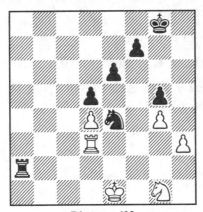

Diagram 498

Black's final step is to activate his king. It's practically over.

> **25. Kf1 Kg7 26. Re3 Kg6 27. Rd3 f6 28. Re3 Kf7**
> **29. Rd3 Ke7 30. Re3 Kd6 31. Rd3 Rf2+**

32. Ke1 Rg2 33. Kf1 Ra2 34. Re3 e5

Diagram 499

35. Rd3 exd4 36. Rxd4 Kc5 37. Rd1 d4
38. Rc1+ Kd5, White resigns.

Summary: Multi-piece endings are based on the rules of simpler endings, but offer another layer of strategy. As usual, the bishop pair is normally an advantage in open positions, especially with passed pawns on the board. As you're accustomed to reading, knights can excel in closed and blocked positions. More space to move and regroup can be a tangible advantage. Because a single advantage, such as a weak pawn in your enemy camp, is frequently not enough to win, creating an additional weakness that overtaxes the defense is a practical technique in many endings. And remember, endgames with several pieces on the board can quickly boil down to simpler positions. It's usually good to place your king in or near the center, but you must use discretion to keep him out of any real danger.

Anatoly Karpov, the 12th World Champion, claimed the throne when Bobby Fischer would not show up for their scheduled 1975 match.

Karpov, an unsurpassed endgame genius, lost his title to Kasparov, but once again became the official FIDE champion after Kasparov bolted to form a series of separate organizations.

Karpov remains one of the most successful tournament players of all time.

Photo by Bill Hook. Courtesy USCF.

ENDGAMES WITH SEVERAL PIECES ON EACH SIDE BOIL DOWN TO SIMPLER ONES. YOU SHOULD CAREFULLY CONSIDER WHICH EXCHANGES BENEFIT EACH SIDE. USUALLY IT'S ADVANTAGEOUS TO KEEP YOUR KING IN THE CENTER, BUT YOU NEED TO USE DISCRETION ON THIS POINT, SINCE WITH A NUMBER OF PIECES STILL ON THE BOARD, HIS MAJESTY CAN BECOME THE VICTIM OF HARASSMENT.

Multi-Piece Endings
Learning Exercises

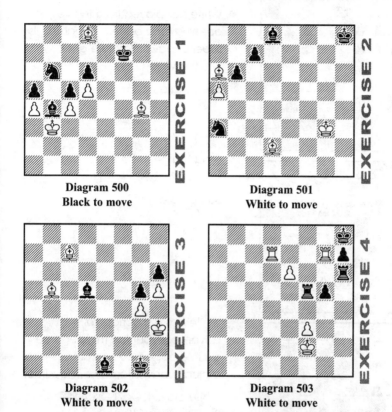

Diagram 500
Black to move

EXERCISE 1

Diagram 501
White to move

EXERCISE 2

Diagram 502
White to move

EXERCISE 3

Diagram 503
White to move

EXERCISE 4

Multi-Piece Endings
Solutions

No. 1 **1. ... Ke8 2. Bxb6 Ke7** = (a rare type of fortress).

No. 2 **1. Bc3+ Kg8 2. Bc4+ Nxc4 3. a6 b5 4. Ba5 +-.**

No. 3 **1. Bb6+** (1. Bh2+ Kh1 2. Bf1 Bd2 3. Bc7 Kg1 4. Ba6 Bg2+ 5. Kg3 Be1 #) **1. ... Kh1 2. Bf2 Bb4** (2. ... Bxf2 3. Bc6 =) **3. Bf1 Bd6 4. Be3 Bh2 5. Bd4 Bg1 6. Bxg1 Kxg1 7. Bd3 Kf2 8. Bf5 =.**

No. 4 **1. e7 Re6** (1. ... Re5 2. Rxg5) **2. Rxh7+ Kg8 3. Rg7+ Kh8 4. Rg6 Ree5 5. Rc6 +-.**

Transitions
Some Important Ideas to Look For

◆ White has played from the very opening for a better endgame. His superior pawn structure gives him the win.

See Diagram 506.

◆ Black's urge to centralize with 1. ... Ke7? loses!

See Diagram 511.

◆ White has a big material advantage, but the middlegame is double-edged. So he transposes to a clearly advantageous endgame.

White plays 1. Qc7! Qxe4 2. Qf4. See Diagram 519.

◆ Black employs an unorthodox but correct transition to an endgame.

Black plays 1. ... Nd7 2. Rd1 Nxc5 3. Rxd3 Nxd3. See Diagram 534.

Chapter 11
Transitions:

Entering the Endgame with Intent

T he endgame isn't, of course, a game of its own. It's the last lap of the race for victory.

Whether you find yourself a few steps ahead or a half-lap behind, the endgame you face is a logical result of the other two stages of chess—the opening and middlegame. There are many moments during these other phases when a player must consider dissolving forces and moving into the endgame, or decide to avoid such a transition. Frequently a player chooses a plan or even specific moves because he intends to enter an ending. In such cases, his middlegame, and even opening, strategy shows its merit in the endgame.

PLAYING FOR A FAVORABLE ENDING FROM MOVE FOUR

There are some openings that are favorites for those who want to enter an endgame quickly. The Exchange variation of the Ruy Lopez is one. The following game brings to mind the famous St. Petersburg, 1914, clash between the two great endgame masters, world champions Emanuel Lasker and Jose Capablanca. Needing a win against his would-be successor, later seen as the greatest, most confident endgame player ever, Lasker chose this variation as White—and won the endgame! The following game more clearly illustrates our theme, although you should play over the classic Lasker-Capablanca game at some point to see two of the world's greatest argue the same ideas. Their battle is anthologized in many, many books.

After the opening moves:

> **1. e4 e5 2. Nf3 Nc6 3. Bb5 a6 4. Bxc6 dxc6**
> **5. Nc3 Bd6 6. d4 Bg4?**

we reach the following position.

LUBLINSKY—ERUHIMOV
RUSSIA, 1960

Diagram 504

With 4. Bx6 and 6. d4, White has already shown his intention— just a few moves into the struggle—of switching to an endgame

with an extra pawn on the kingside. Black has an extra pawn on
the queenside, but because it's doubled, it can't be used to create a passed pawn. Take all the pieces off the board, and White
should win the pawn ending! So Black should try to avoid
exchanges while giving his bishop pair some space to be effective. His last move, leading to the exchange of one of these
bishops, is a serious mistake—it only serves to forward his
opponent's plan.

**7. dxe5 Bxf3 8. Qxf3 Bxe5 9. Bf4 Qf6 10. Bxe5 Qxe5
11. Qe3 Rd8?!**

Black would have better chances to defend with 11. ... Ne7 and
12. ... 0-0.

12. f4

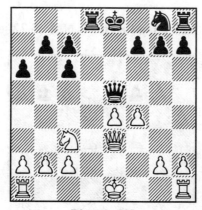

Diagram 505

12. ... Qd4?

Black makes it easy for White to dissolve forces. Before allowing the most powerful piece to come off the board, a player
should consider the resulting position carefully. Here Black
should play 12. ... Qe7.

**13. Qxd4 Rxd4 14. Rd1! Rxd1+ 15. Kxd1 Nf6 16. Ke2
Ke7 17. Rd1 Rd8? 18. Rxd8 Kxd8**

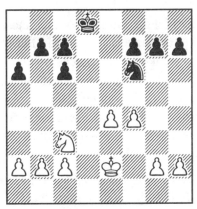

Diagram 506

White has been playing purposefully, while Black's actions were a series of misjudgments. The resulting position is won for White.

19. Kf3 Ke7 20. g4 Ke6 21. Ne2 c5 22. e5 Nd5 23. Ke4

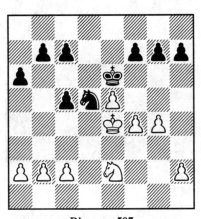

Diagram 507

23. ... Nb6

In case of 23. ... Nb4 24. c3 Nxa2, the knight would be lassoed after 25. f5+ Kd7 26. Kd3 Kc6 27. Nf4 and Kd3-c2-b1.

24. f5+ Ke7 25. h4 c6 26. g5 g6 27. f6+ Kd7 28. Nf4 Na4 29. e6+ fxe6

Diagram 508

30. h5! gxh5 31. g6 hxg6 32. Nxg6 Ke8 33. Ke5 Nb6

If 33. ... Kf7, 34. Nh8+ and 35. Kxe6 wins.

Diagram 509

34. Kxe6 Nd7 35. f7+ Kd8 36. c4 b5 37. b3 b4 38. Kd6!, Black resigns.

Diagram 510

Here's another example, from a different opening, of heading early for an advantageous endgame, where it is easy for the defender to make fatal mistakes. Alexander Alekhine, here in his successful rematch with Dutchman Max Euwe, was universally feared for his combinational prowess in the middlegame. Euwe avoids this stage of the game, but finds Alekhine to be just as ruthless in the game's final stage.

> **1. Nf3 d5 2. c4 e6 3. d4 Nf6 4. Nc3 c5 5. cxd5 Nxd5 6. g3 cxd4 7. Nxd5 Qxd5 8. Qxd4 Qxd4 9. Nxd4 Bb4+ 10. Bd2 Bxd2+ 11. Kxd2 Ke7?**

ALEKHINE—EUWE
HOLLAND, 1937, WORLD CHAMPIONSHIP MATCH 24TH GAME

Diagram 511

White will organize a queenside attack, in which the leading role goes to his bishop on g2. From there this one attacker's control over the long diagonal confines the movement of three of Black's pieces—the rook on a8, the bishop on c8, and the knight on b8. The move 11. ... Ke7 is a mistake here. Clearly better is 11. ... Bd7 12. Bg2 Nc6 13. Nxc6 Bxc6 14. Bxc6+ bxc6 15. Rac1 0-0-0+ 16. Ke3 Kc7, when White would enjoy just a minimal advantage.

12. Bg2 Rd8 13. Ke3 Na6

Diagram 512

This awkward post of Black's knight is a consequence of 11. ... Ke7. The complications after 13. ... e5 aren't appetizing either because of 14. Nb3 Nc6 15. Rac1 Bd7 16. Nc5.

14. Rac1 Rb8 15. a3 Bd7 16. f4 f6 17. Be4!

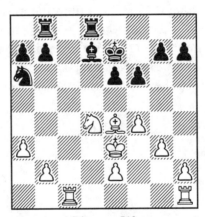

Diagram 513

White prevents 17. ... e5 because he would now have 18. fxe5 fxe5 19. Nf3. At the same time, White spotlights Black's second weakness—the kingside pawns.

17. ... Be8 18. b4

White threatens 19. b5.

18. ... Rd7 19. f5!

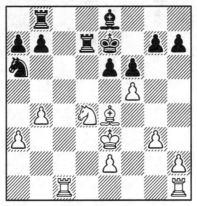

Diagram 514

19. ... Nc7

Forced, although it leads to a loss of a pawn. Black couldn't play 19. ... e5 because of 20. Ne6, with the dual threats of 21. b5 and 21. Nxg7. Neither was 19. ... exf5 a good option because of 20. Bxf5 Rd5 21. Bxh7.

20. fxe6 Nxe6 21. Nxe6 Kxe6 22. Bxh7

An extra pawn gives White a good chance to win.

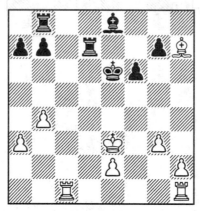

Diagram 515

22. ... f5 23. Rc5 g6 24. Bg8+ Kf6 25. Rhc1 Re7+ 26. Kf2 Bc6

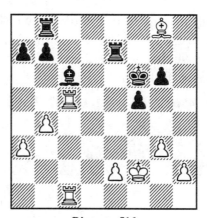

Diagram 516

27. Bd5 Rbe8 28. Re1 Bxd5 29. Rxd5 g5 30. Rd6+ Ke5

Black could put up a bit stronger resistance with 30. ... Kf7. After 30. ... Ke5, his king is overexposed. With several enemy pieces on the board, too much centralization can be dangerous!

31. Red1 g4

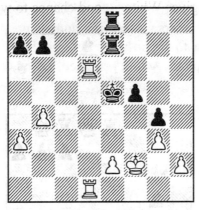

Diagram 517

32. R1d5+ Ke4 33. Rd4+ Ke5 34. Ke3 Re6
35. R4d5+ Kf6+ 36. Kf4 Kg6 37. Rxe6+ Rxe6
38. Re5 Ra6 39. Rxf5 Rxa3 40. Rb5 b6
41. Kxg4, Black resigns.

Diagram 518

If 41. ... Re3, then 42. Rg5+ Kh6 43. b5! Rxe2 44. h4.

You can choose to dissolve the middlegame into an endgame for a variety of reasons—to bring home a positional or material advantage, or to simplify the defense. But you must first be sure you want the endgame you choose. You can't go back!

TSESHKOVSKY—GELLER
VILNIUS, 1980

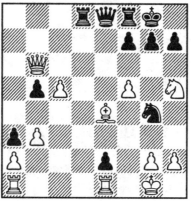

Diagram 519
White to move

Here White has a large material advantage. But an attempt to make use of it in the middlegame is very dangerous. After 1. Ng3, his opponent can play 1. ... Qe5, threatening both 2. ... Qxa1 and 2. ... Qd4+. After 1. Rxe2, 1. ... Qe5 is a killer. Tseshkovsky decides to give back a piece to reach a clearly favorable endgame, thanks to a strong passed pawn on c5.

1. Qc7! Qxe4 2. Qf4 Rfe8

Or 2. ... Qxf4 3. Nxf4, with 3. ... Rd4 4. g3 Rc8 5. Rac1.

3. Qxe4 Rxe4 4. Ng3 Re5 5. Rac1

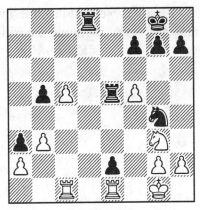

Diagram 520

5. ... Kf8

If 5. ... Rd2, then 6. c6 Re8 7. Rxe2!. Big changes have occurred in the character of the confrontation. Black's former activity has disappeared with the piece exchanges, while White's c-pawn greatly increases in value.

6. Rxe2 Rxe2 7. Nxe2 Ke7 8. c6 Ne5 9. Nd4 b4

If 9. ... Rxd4, then 10. c7.

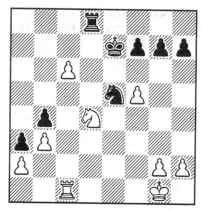

Diagram 521

10. c7 Rc8 11. Nb5 Kd7 12. Rd1+ Ke7 13. Rd4 Nc6 14. Rc4 Kd7 15. Rxc6!, Black resigns.

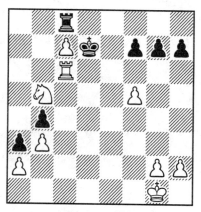

Diagram 522

After 15. ... Kxc6 16. Na7+ Kxc7 17. Nxc8 Kxc8 18. Kf2 Kc7 19. Ke3 Kc6 20. Kd4 Kb5 21. Kd5, White has an easy win in the resulting pawn ending.

Diagram 523
Black to move

In this complicated position, Black's chances would be better if he could exchange queens. Two minor pieces complement the queen so much that exchanging the Lady in this kind of a position is the equivalent of losing a pawn. Black would also improve his chances by advancing and activating his queenside pawns. To do this, he temporarily sacrifices a pawn.

1. ... c5! 2. Qxd5 c4 3. Qxd6 Rxd6 4. Bc2 Rd2

Winning back a pawn.

5. Be4 Rxa2 6. g4 Kg7 7. Bc6 Rd2 8. g5 Rd6 9. Bb7 a5 10. Kg2

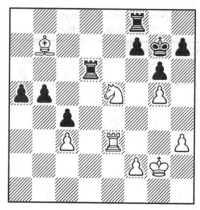

Diagram 524

**10. ... a4 11. Bc6 f6 12. gxf6+ Rdxf6 13. f3 a3
14. Re2 Re6 15. Bxb5 Rf5, White resigns.**

*A follower of
Tarrasch's principles,
Akiba Rubinstein
(1882-1961) was an
endgame wizard who
never got the
financial backing
necessary to
challenge Lasker.
Suffering from
paranoia in his later
years, he died
in reduced
circumstances.*

Courtesy www.chesscafe.com

BOTVINNIK—SOROKIN
MOSCOW, 1931

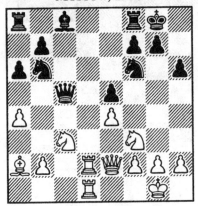

Diagram 525
White to move

White's positional advantage is pretty obvious. But it is not clear how to use the open d-file and how to organize an attack on the precariously located knight on b6 and the pawn on e5. Black's queen protects those weaknesses for now. That's why White decides to exchange queens even at the cost of creating isolated, doubled pawns for himself.

1. Qe3! Qxe3

If 1. ... Qc7, then 2. Nxe5.

2. fxe3 Bg4 3. a5 Nc8 4. Rc1 Bxf3 5. gxf3 Ne7 6. Nd5

The ending ... is concerned to a large extent with the conversion
of an advantage of one pawn into a win.
—Reuben Fine

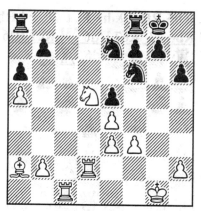

Diagram 526

6. ... Nc6

Or 6. ... Nfxd5 7. Bxd5! Nxd5 8. Rxd5, winning a pawn—for example, if 8. ... f6, then 9. Rc7 Rf7 10. Rxf7 Kxf7 11. Rd7+.

7. Nxf6+ gxf6 8. Rd7 Rab8 9. Kf2 Nxa5
10. Rcc7 Rbc8 11. Rxf7 Rxc7 12. Rxc7+ Kh8 13. Bd5

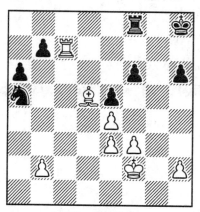

Diagram 527

White's pieces dominate the game. The most logical way for him to win is to transfer his king to h5.

13. ... b5 14. b3 Rd8 15. Kg3 f5 16. Kh4 fxe4 17. fxe4

**Rd6 18. Kh5 Rf6 19. h3 Rd6 20. h4 Rb6 21. Kg4 Rf6
22. Ra7 Rb6 23. Re7 Rd6 24. Rc7 Rf6 25. Ra7 Rb6
26. Rc7 Rf6 27. Kh5 Rd6**

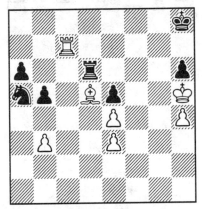

Diagram 528

Now White finally goes for the kill.

**28. Bf7! Rf6 29. Bg6 Nxb3 30. Kxh6 Rf8 31. Rxh7+
Kg8 32. Rg7+ Kh8 33. Bf7 Rxf7 34. Rxf7 Kg8 35.
Kg6 Nd2 36. Rd7, Black resigns.**

HEADING FOR THE ENDGAME AS A DEFENSIVE MEASURE

As we've said, making the transition to an endgame can be a successful defensive strategy. When the middlegame is too hot to handle, and the ending looks defensible, a master will search for a way to get the heavy-hitters off the board.

SMYSLOV—KERES
MOSCOW, 1941

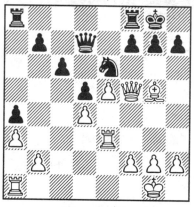

Diagram 529
Black to move

Black is in a dangerous position. White threatens to begin a powerful attack with Rh3 or Bf6. So Black plays a move that encourages the exchange of queens.

1. ... Nc5! 2. g4?

This is a serious mistake. It is better to play 2. Qxd7 Nxd7 3. e6, with equality; or 2. Qc2 Ne4 3. Bh4 Qg4 4. Rh3, with mutual chances. Now, White gets a worse ending.

2. ... Qxf5 3. gxf5 f6!

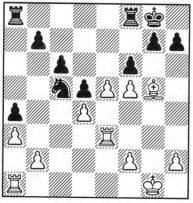

Diagram 530

4. exf6

Other continuations are even worse: 4. Bxf6 Ne4 5. Bh4 Rxf5; or 4. Bf4 Nb3 5. Rd1 fxe5; or 4. dxc5 fxg5 5. Rf3 g6 6. f6 Kf7 and 7. ... Ke6.

4. ... Ne4 5. fxg7 Rxf5 6. Be7 Kxg7

Black has pressure on the kingside files, and his knight is stronger than White's bishop.

7. f3 Nd2 8. Kf2 Re8 9. Rae1

White now threatens 10. Bf6+.

9. ... Ne4+ 10. Kg2

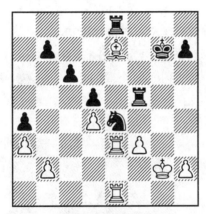

Diagram 531

10. ... Rxe7 11. fxe4 Rxe4 12. Rxe4 dxe4 13. Rxe4 Rb5 14. Re2 Rb3!

Diagram 532

White's king is cut off, and his pawns on b2, d4 and h2 are weak. Black has good chances to win.

15. Kf2 Kf6 16. Ke1 h6 17. Rg2 Ke6 18. Kd1

The try 18. Rg6+ fails because of 18. ... Kd5 19. Rxh6 Rxb2.

18. ... Kd5 19. Kc2

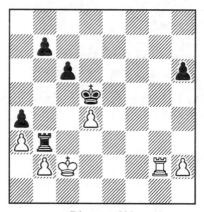

Diagram 533

19. ... Rh3 20. Rd2 Kc4 21. Kb1 h5 22. Ka2 Rh4 23. Rf2 Kxd4

Black, with an extra pawn and more active pieces, went on to win.

GELLER—KROGIUS
BAD WORISHOFEN, GERMANY, 1991

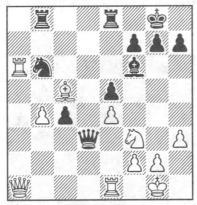

Diagram 534
Black to move

White has a significant positional advantage. His bishop is more active. He's doubled heavy pieces to control the open a-file. In general, his pieces have more space. In case of 1. ... Nc8 2. Re3 Qd7 3. Qc1, Black loses his c4 pawn. So Black finds a queen sacrifice to force a transition into a safe endgame.

1. ... Nd7 2. Rd1 Nxc5 3. Rxd3 Nxd3 4. Rc6 Rxb4 5. Nd2 Nb2 6. Qa5 Rbb8

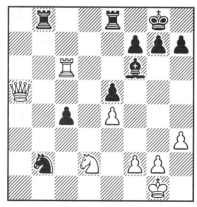

Diagram 535

7. Nxc4 Nxc4 8. Rxc4 h6 9. g3 Rec8 10. Rxc8 Rxc8 11. Kg2 Re8

Diagram 536

Two important facts are in the defender's favor: all the pawns are on the same side and all White's minor pieces are exchanged. Black easily defends his fortress.

12. Qb5 Kf8 13. Qc6 Re6 14. Qc8+ Re8 15. Qf5 Kg8 16. h4 Re6 17. h5 Be7

Diagram 537

18. Qf3 Bf6 19. Qd3 Re8 20. Qb5 Kf8 21. Qc5+ Kg8 22. f4 Re6 23. Qc8+ Kh7 24. Kf3 Re7 25. Qf8 Rc7 26. Kg4 Re7 27. Kf5 Ra7

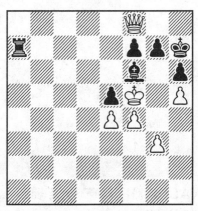

Diagram 538

28. fxe5 Ra5 29. Qxf7 Rxe5+ 30. Kf4 Rg5 31. Qe8 Bc3 32. g4 Bf6 33. Qb8 Bd4, draw.

Summary: The endgame isn't a game by itself, but rather the result of the opening and middlegame. Many times during the middlegame, you have to consider the consequences of forcing or allowing transition to an endgame. Sometimes even an opening has the ultimate goal of producing a favorable endgame. You can choose to go into the endgame as a way of consolidating your advantage or of simplifying a difficult defense. But once in an ending, you can't go back again! So consider transitions thoughtfully.

RELATIVE VALUE OF THE QUEEN VERSUS TWO ROOKS:

- ♚ IN THE MIDDLEGAME, THEY'RE EQUAL.
- ♚ THE QUEEN IS SOMEWHAT WEAKER IN THE ENDGAME.
- ♚ WITH NO OTHER PIECES ON THE BOARD, TWO ROOKS OFTEN EQUAL QUEEN AND PAWN.

The Relative Value of the Pieces Change in the Endgame!

Before you decide to exchange queens and head for an endgame, you should consider the changes that take place in the relative value of the pieces. The power of pawns and rooks grows, and, to a lesser extent, the bishop's power likewise increases. A sort of "net sum" of the power of all pieces is maintained, however, as the knight loses power. Even the queen decreases a bit in its *relative* strength.

OPENING AND MIDDLEGAME PIECE VALUES

In the opening and middlegame, a rook and two pawns are at best equal to two minor pieces. More specifically, rook and two pawns are:

♚ clearly weaker than two bishops;

♚ equal to or slightly weaker than bishop and knight;

♚ equal to two knights.

ENDGAME PIECE VALUES

In the endgame, however, a rook and a single pawn are:

♚ equal to two knights;

♚ equal or slightly weaker than bishop and knight.

The bishop pair is the toughest customer for the rook in an endgame; partially because the bishops also increase in value. But even compared to the bishops, the rook's relative value increases more.

♚ A rook and two pawns are generally the equal of the bishop pair in the endgame.

GUIDELINES FOR EXCHANGING

Keep these tips in mind—they hold true in a vast majority of positions:

♚ When a queen and two minor pieces take on a queen and rook, the side with minor pieces for the rook should avoid exchanging queens. The value of the minor-piece duo decreases after the trade of queen, in fact the exchange often amounts to losing a pawn.

♚ A player with two rooks against a rook and a minor piece—or against a rook and two minor pieces—should exchange his "redundant" rook for his opponent's lone rook. Since the rook's power is unique, one side is thus left with the special power of the piece, and the other side loses it completely.

These guidelines for exchanging hold true no matter how many pawns, or what other sets of pieces, are present on the board.

Transitions
Learning Exercises

Diagram 539
White to move

Diagram 540
Black to move

Diagram 541
Black to move

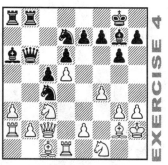

Diagram 542
Black to move

Transitions
Solutions

No. 1 **1. Qxf7+! Qxf7 2. Bxf7+!!** (2. Rxf8+? Kxf8 3. Bxf7 Bc5 =)
2. ... Kxf7 3. Rxf8+ Kxf8 4. Kxf2 (White is clearly much better
because of his potential outside passed pawn) **4. ... Ke7 5. Ke3
Kd6 6. Ke4 b4 7. c3 b3 8. c4 g6 9. g4 h5 10. gxh5 gxh5 11. h4
Kc6 12. Kxe5 Kc5 13. Kf5!** (triangulation)

Diagram 543
Black to move

13. ... Kd4 14. Kf4 Kc5 15. Ke5 Kxc4 16. Ke4 Kc5 17. Kd3 +-.

No. 2 **1. ... Qc3!**, exchanging all pawns and transferring into a queen vs.
rook endgame, and therefore a win. Tempting but wrong would be
1. ... Qxb4 2. axb4 axb3 3. Kb2 Kc4 4. Ka3 b2! 5. Ka2! =.

No. 3 **1. ... dxe5! 2. Nxe5 Bxe5! 3. dxe5 Qxd1+ 4. Kxd1 Nc6** (∓)
5. Nd2 Bf5! (to provoke 6. g4 and thus saddle White with two
weaknesses—on g4 and, potentially, on f4) **6. g4 Be6 7. f4 0-0-0
8. b3 Nd4!**, with a big advantage.

No. 4 **1. ... Qb3! 2. Be4 Qxc2 3. Bxc2 Nxb2! 4. Bxb2 Bc4 5. Rda1
Rxb2! 6. Rxb2 Bxc3 7. Rb7 Bxa1 8. Rxd7 Bxe2 9. Nd2 Rxa3
10. Rxe7 Ra2 11. Rxe2 Rxc2** with a decisive edge for Black.

Conclusion

Knowledge is power. In the case of chess endings, this knowledge is a power that leads to better results!

You've just completed a study of all endgame knowledge essential to your chess for the rest of your life. After all, chess endgame principles don't change. Given the frequency and importance of the endgame, the time and energy you've spent will be a rewarding investment. But there are things you should continue to do both to retain your newfound knowledge and to gain an even deeper understanding of chess endgames.

First of all, regularly reviewing this book is important. The color-coding of the most important positions and ideas makes the process easy. We encourage you to circle, underline, and make your own comments in the margins as you do this.

Secondly, connect your own experiences with this book. Keep this book in your chess bag. Your interest is at its peak immediately after you've finished an intriguing endgame. Use the table of contents to find where the general principles of your game are discussed. Do the principles given apply, or is your position an exception or addition? You may want to draw or paste the new position into the closest blank space.

Collecting and sorting your own endgames is a very important step to your ongoing improvement. We suggest keeping files (on paper or on computer) of the different types of endings you play. The divisions we suggest in this book should work well.

In addition, you could keep another file separating your endings by themes—zugzwang, bad bishop, reserve pawn moves, etc. Again, the themes we suggest in this book should work well as your divisions or subtopics. Each time you play another interesting endgame, use your files to compare it with your previous ones of the same type or theme. You'll be surprised and gratified how quickly you gain confidence and knowledge—and how well your increased understanding sticks with you!

In every phase of your chess study, recognize the importance of endgame play. When you play over a master game, don't quit as soon as one player has a winning advantage, play all the moves out! You need to see how the masters convert their advantages to wins!

Finally, keep in mind that winning endgame play requires planning. Don't just think in terms of what moves are immediately available, *plan*. Don't just play, *build*!

You'll love the results, and you'll love being a player *no one* likes getting into an endgame with!

A Brief Endgame
Glossary

Page numbers given in *italics*.

Breakthrough: Creating a far-advanced passed pawn with a sacrifice. *74*

Building a bridge: Winning technique in the Lucena position. *143*

Chenturini's Rule: In same colored bishop endgames, defender draws if his bishop always has an available safe move on the short diagonal. *210*

Counting: A method of determining if a passed pawn will safely promote. *34*

Distant Passed Pawn: A passed pawn far away from the other pawns. *65*

Endgame: The stage of the game in which so many pieces have been captured that the kings can take an active part in the battle and passed pawns assume extra importance. *11*

Long Diagonal: The longer of two key diagonals in bishop endgames.

Long Side: In rook and pawn endings, refers to the number of files between the pawn and the edge of the board. The long side has more squares than the short side. *146*

Lucena Position: A specific type of rook and pawn vs. rook position in which the strong side "builds a bridge" with his king, rook and pawn to win. *143*

Major Pieces: The rooks and queen.

Minor Pieces: The bishops and knights.

Moving Screen: Taking a short route with your king while forcing the enemy king into a longer route. Also called "running screen," "running pick" or "shouldering." *56*

Mutual Defense Treaties: When pawns (or pawn and knight) defend each other because if one is captured, the remaining pawn queens. *69*

Opposition: When the kings oppose each other with one square between, the side that does not have to move "has the opposition." *38*

Passed Pawn: A pawn with no enemy pawns to block or capture it. *64*

Passing the Move: Giving the move back to your opponent. *52*

Promotion: When a pawn reaches the final row on the opposite side of the board, it has the option of becoming a queen, rook, bishop or knight.

Philidor's Position: A famous rook versus rook-and-pawn draw. *140*

Queening: Promoting a pawn to a queen.

Safe Square: In king-and-pawn endings, any square on which the defending king can stand to maintain the draw. *51*

Short Diagonal: The shorter of two key diagonals in bishop endgames.

Short Side: In rook and pawn endgames, refers to the number of files between the pawn and the edge of the board. The short side has fewer squares than the long side. *149*

Square of the Pawn: A technique to quickly calculate whether an unprotected pawn can queen. It's an imaginary square that contains the same number of chessboard squares as the number of moves it will take the pawn to promote. Also called the Berger Square. *34*

Targeting: Attacking a pawn to force it to the wrong color square or tie the enemy king to its defense. *244*

Triangulation: A technique to pass the move. The king takes two moves to get to a square he could have gone to in one move, thus giving the appearance of tracing a triangle. *62*

Under-promotion: Pawn promotion to a rook, bishop, or knight.

Zugzwang: German for "compulsion to move."

The right 7 books that can make you a Chess Champ!

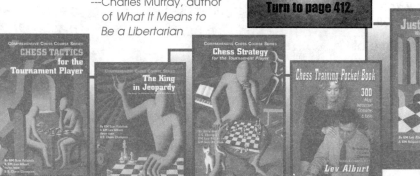

Whether you play chess for fun or chess for blood...

Whether you're a casual player or a tournament veteran... You're invited to join America's coast-to-coast chess club!
We're the U.S. Chess Federation, with over 85,000 members of all ages —from beginners to grandmasters!

U.S. Chess Federation membership offers many benefits:

- The right to earn a national rating!
- A national magazine packed with information
- The right to play in local, regional, and national tournaments
- Big discounts on chess merchandise
- An official membership card
- The right to play officially rated chess by mail

☑ *Yes! Enroll me as follows:*

❏ Adult $40/Yr. ❏ Senior *(age 65 or older)* $30/yr. ❏ Youth *(age 19 and under; includes monthly* Chess Life*)* $17/yr.
❏ Scholastic *(age 14 and under; includes bimonthly School Mates)* $12/yr.
❏ Also, I want my FREE *Play Chess* video (a $19.95 value). I will include $4.50 to cover shipping and handling costs.
❏ Send me *Play Chess I* (Covers the basics, plus winning strategic tips.) **OR**
❏ *Play Chess II* (Takes beginners who know the moves all the way to their first tournament.)

Check or money order enclosed, in the amount of $_____or charge it.

Credit card number_____ Expiration date _____

Authorized signature _____Daytime telephone _____

Name _____Address _____

City _____ State _____ ZIP _____

Birthdate _____ Sex _____

Call toll free: 800-388-KING (5464) Please mention Dept. 11 when responding. **FAX:** 914-561-CHES(2437) or **Visit our website at http://www.uschess.org. Mail:** U.S. Chess Federation, Dept. 11, 3054 NYS Route 9W, New Windsor, NY 12553
Note: Membership dues are not refundable. Canada: Add $6/yr. for magazine postage & handling. Other foreign: Add $15/yr.